D0252267

# LIGHT FOR
# MY PATH
## for
# Teachers

# LIGHT FOR
# MY PATH
## for
# Teachers

## Illuminating Selections
## from the Bible

Pamela Kaye Tracy

HUMBLECREEK
INSPIRATION FOR LIFE

Cover image © PhotoDisc

Published by Barbour Publishing, Inc., P.O. Box 719, Uhrichsville, Ohio 44683, www.barbourbooks.com

*Our mission is to publish and distribute inspirational products offering exceptional value and biblical encouragement to the masses.*

Printed in the United States of America.
5 4 3 2 1

# DEDICATION

*To the students and staff at*
*Paradise Valley Community College.*

# CONTENTS

# PREFACE

A teacher's day does not begin at nine and end at five. A teacher wakes up planning, drives to school fine-tuning the plans, and walks into a day where plans always change because students are ever changing. How blessed is the teacher who knows God is by his or her side and included in his or her plans. *Light for My Path for Teachers* touches on some of the situations facing today's teachers. There is nothing new under the sun, but knowing that across the nation many teachers face the same conflicts and comforts and that a multitude of teachers are praying is one of God's truest blessings.

This book is designed for teachers who both plan and pray. In education, every situation is unique, but chances are in this book you'll find concerns that mirror your own. Take each situation, add to it, edit it, and experience it with the attitude that Jesus is working with you.

They say that teaching is a triangle between parent, child, and teacher. Teachers make bulletin boards dedicated to this idea. *Light for My Path for Teachers* grasps this concept and highlights the final, most important element of the triangle—the center. And in the center is God.

# ASSESSMENT ANXIETY

*"To one he gave five talents of money,*
*to another two talents,*
*and to another one talent,*
*each according to his ability."*

MATTHEW 25:15

Who am I, Lord, to have such tremendous responsibility? I am supposed to assign a letter grade evaluating each student's abilities. How I wish all students were measured with only multiple choice and true/false tests. Then I'd have something tangible to hold before the parents. "Look," I'd say. "It's here in black and white. It has nothing to do with my assessment of his abilities. He missed number four." Instead, I agonize over the gray areas—the essay questions, the science project, the oral presentation. This child, Lord, he's one of Yours. He's struggling. Help him. Oh, help him, Lord. And please help me reach him. Help me to find the method, the tools, to guide and inspire him.

# And the Little Children Shall Lead

*The disciples, each according to his ability,*
*decided to provide help for*
*the brothers living in Judea.*

Acts 11:29

I've just finished giving a lesson, Lord. The students look at me with different expressions. Some are nodding. Some are thinking. Others are confused. What is the best method for reaching them? Why do I think I'm the only one who can do it all? Lord, remind me that it's often a peer who can, with the simplest of words, explain a difficult concept. Lord, remind me not to rush through lessons. Remind me not only to encourage questions, but also to allow others to give the answers. Remind me to let the little children take on the role of teacher. These precious ones are often more perceptive than I. They speak a different language, the language of contemporaries. And, Lord, help me to cherish the lessons I learn from them.

# THE MEASUREMENT OF A CHILD

*But remember the* LORD *your God,*
*for it is he who gives you*
*the ability to produce wealth.*

DEUTERONOMY 8:18

Who says wealth is money? Lord, I say wealth should be measured by how many hugs one receives in a day. No, even better than that, I say wealth is receiving hugs from someone who has disappointed you and someone you have disappointed. Father, we are all Your children, and You've given us different abilities. In children, You've given the ability to love, forgive, and express freely. After a frustrating day, Lord, I am amazed by the students who—no matter what's happened between morning recess and P.E.—think it an honor to hug the teacher good-bye. Never let me take that for granted, Lord. Never let me think about the sweaty fingers, the runny nose, and the dried glue residue. Instead, let me think about the love, trust, and desire to please that guides the student behind the hug. And, Lord, always let me remember to hug back.

# CROSSING THE FINISH LINE

*We were under great pressure,*
*far beyond our ability to endure,*
*so that we despaired even of life.*

2 CORINTHIANS 1:8

Lord, I'm looking forward to meeting Paul. I have lots of questions for him. I cannot even fathom the hardships he suffered. Especially such hardships that made him despair of life. I despair, sometimes, over a struggling child whom I cannot reach. They enter school, Lord, and on the first day, they all stand at a starting line. The teacher blows the horn, and they're off! Some reach the finish line before Christmas, and I wonder why they're in my class. Others run along right on target. Sometimes they gain speed; sometimes they slow down; but they're always reliable. But, Lord, there are always the stragglers. And, no matter how I try; how their parents try; how all the peer tutors, after-school programs, and wonder drugs try; these students suffer. Lord, never let me push them to the breaking point. Always help me to find some new method, some untried avenue, anything to keep them in the race.

# BROTHER, CAN YOU SPARE A DIME?

*Who shall separate us from the love of Christ?*
*Shall trouble or hardship or persecution or*
*famine or nakedness or danger or sword?*

ROMANS 8:35

Father, she's chosen homelessness as her essay topic. She sits in the front row, and if I'd had just a third of her drive as a college student, I'd have saved years of aimless seeking. She's young, too—one of the youngest in the class—so when she tells me that she intends to dress up as a homeless person and panhandle on the street as research for her paper, I discourage her. But she protests...and she assures me that her mother is going with her. I'm still full of misgivings. I wouldn't pretend to be homeless and panhandle on a street corner, even if Arnold Schwarzenegger were going with me. A few days later, I walk into my class, and she's teaching those who arrived early. She made forty dollars an hour, and the class is pretty impressed. I give her all the time she needs. Lord, You had followers like this student. Those who took chances and went places that rich young rulers were afraid to go. I'm still uncomfortable that her essay research took her to a place I consider dangerous—which is why, when she began her research on tattoos, I vetoed a thought I didn't want to cross her mind.

# IN MY FATHER'S FOOTSTEPS

*A wise son heeds his father's instruction.*

PROVERBS 13:1

---

In Study Skills class, Lord, my high school seniors prepare to give presentations. They've done extensive research into the career of their choice. Their classroom goal is to sell themselves to prospective employers. My wannabe teachers role-play the classroom environment. My future lawyers stage mock trials. The soon-to-be firemen stage heroic rescues. And the young man who wants to be a preacher demonstrates what a counseling session might look like; he's videotaped the proceedings in his father's office. He looks so at home! Lord, what a breath of fresh air. Not only does the young man want to be a preacher, but he wants to follow in his father's footsteps. Lord, thank You for that father who made such an impression on his son.

# A GIVING HEART

*"Remembering the words the Lord Jesus himself said:*
*'It is more blessed to give than to receive.' "*

ACTS 20:35

It's the second week of school, and a student in the second row is falling behind, Lord. He has not yet purchased the required textbook. During class, he scoots his chair over and shares. Outside of class, he's not getting his homework done. He already has two zeros in my grade book. There was a time, early in my college teaching career, that I would have loaned him a book. But thanks to textbook changes, stolen books, and my own personal jadedness, I no longer go out of my way to supply unprepared students with books. A woman who sits behind this young man does it for me. "Where's your book?" she asked one day. "I'm waiting for payday," he replied. The next class period she hands him a book and a receipt. "Pay me on payday," she says. I want to pull her aside, warn her it will never happen, and tell her he'll stop attending before payday rolls around. It's a good thing I didn't, because the young man would have proved me wrong. A week later, he hands her the money. Lord, I'm still not impressed by the young man who should have purchased his book with his paycheck *before* classes began. But I am impressed with the woman. She makes me want to work on my jadedness. She has none; I have plenty. Lord, she's a blessing.

# WHO ARE YOU?

*I lift up my eyes to the hills—*
*where does my help come from?*

PSALM 121:1

Father, a fellow English instructor shared the story of a student who stopped by her office wanting help. Dutifully, she sat down and went over his essay. Then off he went. It wasn't until she received his next essay via mail that she realized he wasn't even this semester's student. He was a former student wanting help! Lord, with more than a hundred new students each semester, it's hard to remember who goes where and when. Help us to reach out when we can, guide when we can, and redirect when we can't.

# CLOSE OF DAY

*"He who has ears to hear,
let him hear."*

LUKE 8:8

There are crayons on the floor, Lord. Bits of paper litter the carpet. The contents of one desk blocks the aisle. It is afternoon. My classroom has that lived-in look. I carefully traverse to the front of the room and start writing on the board. The students are finishing a test. Soon they'll shuffle back to my desk, turn in their test papers, and we'll start our final lesson. I always end with a subject I think is a bit more conversational—like history. Three times a week, it's history. Just like Jesus taught with parables, I tell lots of stories. They learn about Benjamin Franklin paying too much for a whistle. They know Thomas Jefferson made a traveling desk. They know the Disney cartoon about Pocahontas has many mistakes. I like to think that they leave my classroom with more knowledge than they had when they entered. Thank You, Lord, for afternoons—when I, too, can be a storyteller.

# To Wriggle or Not to Wriggle

*When he saw the crowds,*
*he had compassion on them,*
*because they were harassed and helpless,*
*like sheep without a shepherd.*

MATTHEW 9:36

Whenever we're doing a school play, Lord, we hold rehearsal in the late afternoon. I suppose we schedule it so the students have something to anticipate. Maybe it's that we know if rehearsals are early, we'd never get the students back into the I-am-student role. I am monitoring those waiting their turn on stage. Hundreds of feet are kicking back and forth in the pews. Wriggling is the name of the game. Hands are waving. Even getting permission to go to the bathroom is better than sitting still. It's afternoon, Lord, and I'd like to escape to the bathroom, too. I cannot lead them in song because that would interfere with practice. Lord, always give me the patience to speak kindly and encourage good behavior as the minutes turn into hours.

# BLESSING IN DISGUISE

*[The LORD] satisfies your desires*
*with good things so that*
*your youth is renewed like the eagle's.*

PSALM 103:5

In the afternoons, Father, I enter the junior high corner of the Christian school where I work. For fifty minutes, I teach history to teenagers who were once my kindergartners. I'm not a junior high teacher at heart. I respect anyone who can spend a whole day with the hormone-laden young people who are struggling between childhood and adulthood. However, teaching history to my old students is a blessing. I hold a special place in their hearts—a place only a past kindergarten teacher can occupy. I knew them when the opposite sex had cooties. I knew them when they couldn't color between the lines. I didn't ask for this blessing, Lord. You just gave it to me. Thank You.

# Loose Ends

*Jesus said, "Take care of my sheep."*

John 21:16

I look at the clock, Lord, and it's inching past one. It's time to send the students to Physical Education. Two by two, I send them to the restroom to change into their gym clothes. I tie shoes; I dry the tears of the student who forgot his P.E. shirt; I send the student with the doctor's note to the office; and I settle behind my desk to answer parent notes, grade papers, and prepare for the rest of the afternoon. There's so much to do. I am human and forgetful. Lord, in the middle of the night, I wake up remembering an item I should have accomplished. Help me to manage my time wisely and see to the needs of my students.

# WHAT A CHILD DESERVES

*"Success, success to you,
and success to those who help you,
for your God will help you."*

1 CHRONICLES 12:18

Wouldn't it be wonderful, Lord, if every time a child entered a classroom, the chant "Success, success to you, and success to those who help you. . ." was playing in the background? Father, so many of these children do not know You. They do not know the You that David knew. Sometimes I feel like I don't know the You that David knew. Oh, how You showed Your love to David. You *helped* him. He succeeded at killing lions, giants, and human enemies. Yet he also loved. He loved his brothers, Jonathan, Bathsheba, but mostly, Lord, he loved You. He made mistakes, but what a full life he lived. People, leaders, gravitated to him. Teach these children to be leaders and not followers. And, if they're followers, Lord, let them follow You.

# PRECIOUS JEWELS

*It shone with the glory of God,
and its brilliance was like that of a very precious jewel,
like a jasper, clear as crystal.*

REVELATION 21:11

Your servant John is speaking of Jerusalem, the Holy City. Sometimes, Lord, there's a student who stands out: a precious jewel who reminds me why I'm a teacher, and why I want to be a teacher forever. I could list the reasons, but every time a student steps past the sacred I-am-teacher-you-are-student line, I'm amazed. I didn't expect this, not from this student. I'd been warned, You see. This student is slow, noisy, and requires lots of extra attention. Lord, I thank You for these precious jewels—the ones who exceed my expectations and become those students who later come back and invite me to their high school graduations. Help me to open myself to all students looking for a mentor. Forgive me for the ones I miss.

# KIDS SAY THE BESTEST THINGS

*Accept one another, then,*
*just as Christ accepted you,*
*in order to bring praise to God.*

ROMANS 15:7

Lord, a new student stood in the doorway of the classroom, and already the odds were stacked against him. He looks different. I'd already been given his folder and knew the story, but the students weren't prepared. I'd agonized over what to do. Should I have mentioned that we were getting a "different-looking" new student? Or should I have not prejudiced them before the boy had a chance to prove his worth? Again, Lord, Your children exceeded my expectations. At recess, there were a few questions, which the boy sounded surprised to be asked, and then the baseball glove went on his hand and the game began. I wish adults bonded as easily and freely. I wish I were as accepting as these children. Differences scare me. I need to let go of my preconceived notions. Help me, Lord, to listen to the interaction of these children and to remember that we *all* are created in Your image.

# THE BEST OF TIMES

*"Woman, you have great faith!*
*Your request is granted."*

MATTHEW 15:28

The primer is in their hands, Lord. They've been memorizing those first sounds: *aah, ay, uh, aw, buh, cuh.* Suddenly, instead of seeing letters, some lucky student sees a word and blurts it out. Everyone looks at him with awe. I squelch the urge to do the happy dance. Oh, all right, I do the happy dance, and for a moment the whole class rejoices. Oh, this is a crowning moment! I tell them from day one that if they try, they'll be reading by the end of the year. And now they *really* believe me. Lord, how many times have You made promises to me and yet I don't believe? Lord, how many times have You blessed me and still I doubt? Thank You, Lord, for granting our requests. Help us to never take You for granted.

# EAGERLY LONGING

*"Let the little children come to me,*
*and do not hinder them,*
*for the kingdom of God belongs to such as these.*
*I tell you the truth,*
*anyone who will not receive the kingdom of God*
*like a little child will never enter it."*

MARK 10:14–15

There are some children who cannot wait to start school, Lord. They long for the smell of paste, the feel of a backpack, the taste of warm water from an outdoor fountain, and the sound of a bell signaling beginnings and ends. They impatiently wait their turn to open the school door and enter a new world. Birthdays, growth charts, new shoes—these are all milestones that take them one step closer to the promised land: school. Lord, I envy their honest anticipation. You bless my life in so many ways, yet I don't seem to anticipate heaven the way these youngsters anticipate the first day of school. How can I change this, Lord? How do I study? I want to experience this type of eagerness. I want everyone to experience it.

# DID I DO IT, TEACHER?!

*Be shepherds of God's flock that is*
*under your care, serving as overseers—*
*not because you must,*
*but because you are willing,*
*as God wants you to be.*

1 PETER 5:2

"I-studied-real-hard-Teacher-honest-I-did-how'd-I-do?" The words escape from the student's lips like the beads from a broken necklace, Father. I'm almost out of breath listening to him. In the younger grades, a big *100%* written at the top of a paper, or a colorful sticker, or best of all—to have the paper displayed on a bulletin board for all to see, is enough motivation. I enjoy their enthusiasm, their quest for approval, and their willingness to try. And, Lord, how I wish that I could always answer the above question with a resounding, "Yes, you got 100 percent!" Lord, help me to strive to give my all to the students who are so eager to learn. Help me to teach them successful strategies while they are still so willing to try. Let me never squelch a desire to learn.

# RITES OF PASSAGE

*But solid food is for the mature.*

HEBREWS 5:14

Father, I know there are certain rites of passage that make parents anticipate. There's the first smile, first solid food, first steps. . . . As a kindergarten teacher, I was privy to the loss of a "first" tooth. Not even Christmas was so charted. A dancing tooth poster in the back of the classroom kept track. If a student lost a tooth in September, he got his name on that month's dancing tooth. If he were so lucky as to lose the tooth in the classroom, he got a plastic tooth locket that sealed the tooth inside. A few children couldn't wait for their teeth to fall out naturally. Oh, how they tugged and wiggled. A few managed to pull out teeth before the gums were willing to surrender. Ouch! Lord, let us enjoy our childhood and let maturity unfold naturally. Let us not be so impatient for the passing of time. Let us cherish the now for what it is.

# AND THE WINNER IS. . .

*"If only I may finish the race
and complete the task the Lord Jesus
has given me. . ."*

ACTS 20:24

Lord, one year our school's spelling-bee winner was a third grader. When we traveled to the district level, he was to go against a battlefield of sixth graders and above. He sat next to me with sweat glistening on his forehead. I could see how excited he was to be here *and* how much he wished he were anywhere else. Anticipation is a funny thing, Lord. We get the same rush whether we look forward to or dread an event. This spelling-bee representative had one wish: He didn't want to be knocked out during the first round. He didn't need to win. He just needed to respect himself for trying. As adults, we are often so afraid of trying because we might fail. I wish I were more like this third grader, willing to fail as long as I can respect myself. Lord, give me the courage to try, especially when I feel like a third grader lost in a battlefield of giants.

# WALKING DOWN HEAVEN'S ROAD

*But everything should be done in
a fitting and orderly way.*

1 CORINTHIANS 14:40

A bell rings to let students and teachers know it is time to change classes, Lord. In a dreamworld, the students traverse the hallway in a fitting and orderly way. In real life, they don't. I've been complained to, and I've been the complainer. I know every trespass: Kindergartners run in the hallways! First graders knock their fists against the walls! Third graders push each other! Junior high students have on headphones! "Fitting and orderly way" is a seemingly unattainable quest. We're like these students, aren't we, Lord? In the hallway of life, we run in directions You've told us not to take. We use our fists when we should turn the other cheek. We push our way impatiently past some of the gentler sides of life. And we're listening to headphones when we should be listening to You. Help us, Lord, to embrace a fitting and orderly way as we travel the hallway of life.

# Taking Joy in the Moment

*"From the lips of children and infants
you have ordained praise."*

Matthew 21:16

Lord, sometimes when I take the end of the jump rope no one notices. Other times, everyone heads over to where a teacher is participating. The little girl jumping is already up to the number twenty-five. The line is thirty children long. She's up to forty. The bell will ring soon, and those at the end will miss their turn. *How do I make it fair?* Lord, I'm glad it's not up to me. I'm worrying, and the children in line are counting. "Fifty-one, fifty-two, fifty-three. . ." They've made it into a singsong. Oh, Father, how many times have I forgotten to enjoy the success of others because I was too worried about my own success? The next time I am sure that someone else is receiving more blessings than I am, I pray You'll remind me to enjoy the blessings. I need to applaud the blessings of others and quit worrying about the bell.

# FOR WHOM THE BELL TOLLS

*Do not forget to entertain strangers,*
*for by so doing some people have*
*entertained angels without knowing it.*

HEBREWS 13:2

The front doorbell buzzes. It's late, Lord, and *I am alone*. Usually, I'm sequestered in my classroom and cannot hear the bell. Not this time. I peer around the corner. Just what I feared: a stranger. My school's not in the best neighborhood. Oh, why didn't I leave at five with everyone else? Why didn't I take my grading home? I approach the door and yell through the glass, "Can I help you?" The man shouts, "I need to use the phone." I can't let him in, Lord. *I am alone*. He's one of Your children, Lord, and he's come for help. "Let me get someone," I shout. Letting myself into the school office, I get on the phone and start off with the minister and work my way through the elders until I find someone who will hurry to help. I wish I were brave enough to help. Lord, please help me know what to do when the bell sounds.

# CHECKS AND BALANCES

*Whoever obeys his command*
*will come to no harm,*
*and the wise heart will know*
*the proper time and procedure.*
*For there is a proper time*
*and procedure for every matter,*
*though a man's misery weighs heavily upon him.*

ECCLESIASTES 8:5–6

Lord, teachers tend to get annoyed when the bell rings and they're not ready. But what if there were no bells! What if we went through life without any checks and balances? The homeroom teacher would take roll and then release her charges—thirty seconds max. My favorite class subject is reading; I'd make it last all day—I'd never teach math or science. The art teacher would only teach watercolors. And, if it were up to the students, the bell on the alarm clock would never ring, nor would a bell signify the end of recess. Thank You, Lord, that life is not a disorganized mess. Thank You, Lord, for teaching us to schedule and to work with each other for the consideration of all.

# SUFFER THE LITTLE CHILDREN

*People will be lovers of themselves,*
*lovers of money, boastful, proud,*
*abusive, disobedient to their parents,*
*ungrateful, unholy.*

2 TIMOTHY 3:2

Last night I ran into a fellow teacher, Lord. I'd not seen her for almost a year. She is a caring, dedicated teacher. Her mother was with her, and the first words from the mother's mouth were: "Tell her about *that* child." For twenty minutes I listened to a frustrated teacher. Lord, we don't mean to dwell with the negative, but often the negative is what we carry home with us. And, Lord, bullies are a concern that we can't seem to resolve. What do we do? Bullies are lost sheep. So we spend more time with them, talk to them, reason with them, and have conferences with their parents. Lord, so often we spend time with the class bully at the expense of the rest of the class. Help us to search for solutions and to deal with the causes as well as the effects.

# THE CHAINS THAT BIND

*So Delilah said to Samson,*
*"Tell me the secret of your great strength*
*and how you can be tied up and subdued."*

JUDGES 16:6

Father, help me to deal with the children who come to school with so much baggage that their anger bubbles over. We see the destruction they leave *externally*: jagged lines etched into desks by sharp objects; torn, wrinkled homework papers; loud voices with sharp edges and belligerent words; manic behavior that follows a restless spirit; and fear in the eyes of the weaker students who want to sit far, far away. Help me to be a teacher who helps to doctor the destruction they have *internally*. Help me to listen and understand. Father, tell me the secret to unlock their heartaches and how their anger can be tied up and subdued.

# My Way or the High Way

*The weapons we fight with are not
the weapons of the world.*

2 Corinthians 10:4

Lord, when we hear the words *school* and *bully* together, the image that often comes to mind is an under-four-foot-tall terror who steals lunches and torments the weak. But teachers know that bullies come in all shapes and sizes. Often the parent of a bully is more of a bully than the child. Also, teachers can be bullies, and certainly there are principals and school-board members who fall into the bully category. Lord, I'm afraid I've even taken on the role of bully when I've wanted something done and needed to spur others into action. Help me, Lord, to understand what a bully is and what bullying does to others. Help me to learn alternative ways to lead.

# JUST WALK AWAY

*"But I tell you, Do not resist an evil person.*
*If someone strikes you on the right cheek,*
*turn to him the other also."*

MATTHEW 5:39

Lord, why is it that I always think it is the weak who are bullied? That is wrong! The Bible specifically tells us to turn the other cheek. It takes a strong individual to resist the temptation to retaliate while being picked on. I think of Jesus being led down the street while bullies called His name. And what did He do? He asked You to forgive them! Lord, I pray for the bullies who don't know how to socialize. I've never met a happy bully. Lord, I pray for the tormented who might dread coming to school. I pray they maintain happiness always. I pray for myself that I may be the kind of teacher who defuses these difficult situations. I desire a happy environment for learning.

# A PERFECT FIT

*The race is not to the swift or*
*the battle to the strong,*
*nor does food come to the wise or*
*wealth to the brilliant or favor to the learned;*
*but time and chance happen to them all.*

I didn't become an elementary teacher by traditional means, Lord. I came through the back door. I became a teacher because a preacher's wife thrust a handful of teaching materials into my arms one night and announced a third-grade opening. Before I could say no, the preacher's wife was gone. The following Wednesday night, I met a woman teaching down the hall. She was also a classroom teacher and wanted to know where I taught during the day. When I told her I was a waitress, she encouraged me to go back to school. She blinked when I told her I already had a degree in journalism and that I made more money waitressing. Through her influence, a year later I found myself in front of a kindergarten classroom. That was more than seventeen years ago, and I'm looking forward to seventeen more. Thank You, Lord, for putting us where we need to be. Thank You, Lord, for guiding me.

# WHEN OPPORTUNITY KNOCKS

*Therefore, as we have opportunity,*
*let us do good to all people,*
*especially to those who belong to the family of believers.*

GALATIANS 6:10

Lord, You know that because of my love of the written word, I took a creative writing course at a nearby community college. The instructor, who later became a close friend of mine, was such a powerful influence that I took the class several times. Later, she and the chair of the English department were putting together a fall schedule and realized they had a Saturday class with no teacher. Brainstorming resulted in my name being figuratively thrown into a hat with no other names. They called me on a Thursday, hired me on a Friday, and I wound up standing in front of college students on a Saturday morning. I taught my first community college class more than eight years ago. It became my second income and freed me from nighttime waitressing. . .and later it segued into a full-time position. Thank you, Lord, for unexpected opportunities.

# THE CHOSEN ONE

*"For many are invited, but few are chosen."*

MATTHEW 22:14

To apply for a full-time college position, Lord, one must put a stack of about twenty papers together—resume, transcripts, letters of recommendation. . . . Knowing the odds of getting hired (about 240 to 1), I applied everywhere. Eventually, I got a call. (Seventeen out of the 240 applicants were phoned for an interview.) This called for a celebration. My husband dutifully took me out to dinner and followed me to the mall to buy a new dark blue suit. I practiced my micro-teaching and practiced answering questions. The day of my interview arrived. I walked down a long hall, was critiqued and questioned by my peers, and went home to await yet another phone call. It came! (Now down to the final 5.) Again I rehearsed answering questions. Finally, I sat before the president of the college and the dean of students. They told me if I got the job, they would call me the following week. I went home and waited for a call that did not come. This called for mourning. I'd been so close! My husband dutifully took me out to dinner but nixed the idea of taking me to the mall to make a sympathy clothes purchase. Turns out he was right; the call came a week after it was supposed to. Lord, waiting to hear good or bad news can be agonizing. Thank You, Lord, for the patience You give me. And thank You for bestowing the gumption to take chances.

# SECONDHAND ROSE

*Many, O LORD my God, are the wonders you have done.*
*The things you planned for us no one can recount to you;*
*were I to speak and tell of them,*
*they would be too many to declare.*

PSALM 40:5

Father, I've been very blessed. I've learned through competition that coming in second is nothing to be shamed of. I've played competitive softball where the second-place trophy was almost as tall as me. I once ran for treasurer of a club and came in second. What a relief, since I can't balance my own checkbook. *(What was I thinking?)* I actually came in second for my dream job. That's right—the position actually went to another individual who turned it down. Lord, coming in second has never been a hindrance. I thank You for the opportunities You've given me. I thank You for seconds.

# RAINY DAYS AND MONDAYS

*When Jesus landed and saw a large crowd,*
*he had compassion on them,*
*because they were like sheep without a shepherd.*
*So he began teaching them many things.*

MARK 6:34

*Recess* is a word teachers love, Lord—unless it's their turn for duty and *it's raining*. In a small school, there are often days when students ranging from age five all the way up to thirteen share the same twenty-minute recess space. If it's not raining, they spread across the playground in groups dependent on age, maturity, and interest. Rain sends us to the gym, where if the teenage girls sit in a corner to chat, the first-grade boys will trip over them while playing catch. If the older boys decide to play basketball, the third-grade girls will not relinquish their favorite jump-roping spot. What should I do in this small, contained space? Jesus fed the masses with just two loaves and five fish. I have two basketball hoops, a ball, and a jump rope. Father, help me on the days when chaos rules. Help me to organize games and keep the students from friction.

# SEEKING THE LOST

*"Suppose a woman has ten silver coins and loses one.*
*Does she not light a lamp, sweep the house*
*and search carefully until she finds it?*
*And when she finds it, she calls her friends*
*and neighbors together and says,*
*'Rejoice with me; I have found my lost coin.' "*

LUKE 15:8–9

The fire alarm sounds, Lord, so I herd my students from the classroom, grab my grade book, close the door, and push the excited students toward the designated area—far enough away from the school for safety. I count my students and come up one short. Panic sets in. Did I send him to the rest room? Is he standing behind someone taller? Turning around, I see him. He's visiting someone else's line! The momentary fear subsides, and relief pours over me. For a moment, he was the most precious student ever to have entered my classroom. These moments happen too often, Lord. I turn around, blink, and a wee one can disappear. Watch over them, Lord, as I—a frail human—cannot. They are Your sheep as I am Your sheep. When we return to the class, we sing songs, play a game, and enjoy a moment of rejoicing.

# IT'S A GOOD THING GOD KNOWS

*"Are not two sparrows sold for a penny?*
*Yet not one of them will fall to the ground*
*apart from the will of your Father."*

MATTHEW 10:29

I don't feel good, Teacher." Quickly, Father, I put my hand to his forehead, then call our secretary—school nurses are a luxury of the past—and pack up my woozy darling. I have my teacher's helper (she's five, and it's a very important duty) accompany the patient to the office. A few minutes later she reports, "The secretary called Mrs. Smith, and she's on her way." Mrs. Smith? Mrs. Smith? That's not good because I didn't send Junior Smith to the office. I sent Junior Jones! Another phone call to the office affirms that the secretary made a mistake. Later, as I settle into the couch for a quiet evening at home, I take my cold tablets, gargle them down with salt water, and realize how blessed I am. Lord, I find it amazing that You never make mistakes. You not only know all our names, but how many hairs are on our heads! What comfort that gives me. I thank You, Lord, that You watch out for me.

# WHERE MANY GATHER

*"How often I have longed to*
*gather your children together,*
*as a hen gathers her chicks under her wings."*

MATTHEW 23:37

Father, one of them is in the office with a fever. Another is in the restroom. Two are waiting their turn for a restroom break; I don't dare send them at the same time—chaos. Father, one of them has a broken shoelace and has been tripping all day. Another lost a button off her shirt; thank You for safety pins—chaos. Two are picking up crayons from the floor, stepping on more than they pick up—chaos. Father, one of them is asleep. Another is falling out of his chair. Two are cleaning the hamster cage; I can't tell You how many times we have lost that hamster—chaos. Father, how wondrous is this life of mine. I watch children all day long. There's no downtime. They keep me hopping, and I feel young with them. Thank You, Father.

# Jesus Loves Me

*" 'Love your neighbor as yourself.'*
*There is no commandment greater than these."*

Mark 12:31

Red and yellow, black and white, they are precious in his sight. . . ."
There's a tossed salad of students in my classroom, Lord, and they
make me a better person. I thank You that we are not all the same. I
thank You for my Hispanic high school girls who bring me pictures
of their *quinceaños*. I thank You for my African-American young
man who proudly wears his ancestral country's colorful attire for the
class photograph. I thank You for my Asian third grader who stands
every time I enter the room. I thank You for my Anglo young man
with a sweet Southern accent. In a classroom, Lord, we can embrace
differences and grow with them.

# ROLE MODELS

*Your beauty should not come from*
*outward adornment, such as braided hair*
*and the wearing of gold jewelry and fine clothes.*
*Instead, it should be that of your inner self,*
*the unfading beauty of a gentle and quiet spirit,*
*which is of great worth in God's sight.*

1 PETER 3:3–4

Today he came as a cowboy, Lord. Yesterday, he was a masked turtle superhero. I wonder what he'll come as tomorrow. As I look across my kindergarten classroom, I see uniformity. Most of my students are dressed in jeans and short-sleeved shirts. A few of the girls are wearing dresses. If I could zap any one of them into a *Brady Bunch* episode, they'd fit right in. Me, too. I am dressed in the guise of a typical teacher: skirt, blouse, and sensible shoes. Not my cowboy, though. Lord, this child makes my day. He is a unique spirit in a world too concerned with sameness and the opinion of others. He has imagination and spunk. He is an individual. Lord, please help him keep these traits always. Keep peer pressure and television from negatively influencing his choice of role models. Lord, I thank You for children who display imagination freely.

# THE PATH TAKEN

*If it is serving, let him serve;*
*if it is teaching, let him teach. . .*
*if it is contributing to the needs of others,*
*let him give generously;*
*if it is leadership, let him govern diligently;*
*if it is showing mercy, let him do it cheerfully.*

ROMANS 12:7–8

They follow behind me, Father. Sometimes I feel like a pied piper. Lord, please help me with this responsibility, because what I've discovered is that it doesn't matter whether they are in preschool, kindergarten, sixth grade, high school, or college, children will follow wherever they are led if they trust the person leading. Help me choose the right way. Help me never forget that the trust of a child is to be cherished.

# ANGELS IN TRAINING

*"For if you forgive men when they sin against you,
your heavenly Father will also forgive you.
But if you do not forgive men their sins,
your Father will not forgive your sins."*

MATTHEW 6:14–15

You know what I like best about children, Lord? The way they forgive. And the way they forget. Why do we lose that trait as we grow older? Why do we keep lists of wrongs and rights? Lord, I watch my class as each day passes by, and I'm amazed by their resilience. In many cases, the parents will carry a grievance a lot longer than a child. I'll get notes from them: "Don't let So-and-So ride in a car with Whozit." Or: "Please move my child's desk so it is no longer near You Know Who." I understand these pleas if the issue is over socializing—in which case, I certainly hope I take care of the problem first. The way we hold on to negative memories worries me, Lord. Especially since I am an adult and carry in my heart my list of wrongs and rights. Let me learn from these children and become a better person.

# READINESS

*Always be prepared to give an answer to*
*everyone who asks you to give the reason*
*for the hope that you have.*
*But do this with gentleness and respect.*

1 PETER 3:15

I listen to talk radio, Father. I find it fascinating. And I'm always glad I'm behind the steering wheel of a car when an education issue is debated. I'm sure I'd call in and say something I'd regret otherwise. One issue was whether kindergartners should be allowed to enter school at 4.8—that's four years and eight months of life. The commentator and the call-ins mostly sided with "Yes." In my experience, most parents who want to start their child before the September 5 cutoff date want to do so for babysitting purposes. It's less expensive to put a child in school than to pay for child care. But I've had four-year-olds in my classroom who *were* ready. Lord, when these issues are debated, let the welfare of the child be the deciding factor, *not* day care.

# ASSIGNED SEATS

*You know when I sit and when I rise;*
*you perceive my thoughts from afar.*

PSALM 139:2

Tonight, Father, as I sat in *my* pew at church, I realized that from childhood I've sat on the right side toward the back. The location says a lot about me. Where students sit in the classroom says a lot about them, too. When I taught kindergarten, I'd place my students boy/girl. When I taught third grade, I'd place my students good influence/bad influence. When I taught sixth grade, I'd place my students mature/immature. Students with poor eyesight were in the front row. Behavior problems were closest to my desk. Now that I teach college, I don't do name tags, and I watch with curiosity as students pick their own places. Some make wise choices: front row. Some make foolish choices: closest to the door and escape. Lord, help us, Your children, make the best choices—be it a seat in the class, saying no to temptation, or saying yes to Your Word.

# THE HARD WAY

*A certain ruler asked him,*
*"Good teacher, what must I do*
*to inherit eternal life?"*

LUKE 18:18

Lord, a certain student asked me, "Good teacher, what must I do to pass your class?"

I replied, "Do not miss class. Do not come to class late. Do not let your cell phone ring. Do your homework." And the student, very bright, very worthy, nodded. This certain student started with good intentions. He enjoyed the lectures, but he missed a few classes. He was often late. On occasion, his cell phone interrupted our class. His homework was done at the last minute and often incomplete. One day, he exceeded the absences allotment and was dropped from the class. Responsibility, commitment, effort—they are so important. Lord, help today's students to appreciate the opportunity afforded to them. And, help me, Father, to make my classroom one that inspires learning.

# By Our Works

*Whatever you do,*
*work at it with all your heart,*
*as working for the Lord, not for men.*

COLOSSIANS 3:23

Today, Lord, a student came to see me. I wish he'd done it sooner in the semester when there was still time to "fix" the problem. He sits there with the evidence—his final grade—in front of him. This student made a choice to disregard quite a few assignments, and now he needs to repeat the class. Not the kind of second chance he really wants. As a young person, it's quite possible he didn't realize that in the "real" world, a student earns grades. He's looking at me—wanting—hoping that a miracle will happen and that I'll make the choice to say, "Oh, never mind. I'll *give* you the grade you want."

Lord, You give me all kinds of second chances. I thank You for them. Please help me make more "right" choices the first time around.

# TURTLES VS. DEER

*In fact, though by this time*
*you ought to be teachers,*
*you need someone to teach you*
*the elementary truths.*

HEBREWS 5:12

We're in the back of the room at the reading table, Lord. I've taught letters, sounds, and punctuation to my primary students. They're ready to put learning to practice. I place them into groups of three to five. They all start at the same place in book 1. The first sentence is: "Let's go to the zoo." For a brief moment in time, my whole class is ready to go to the zoo. And, yet, Lord, in a few months, I'll have some reading groups in book 10. The first sentence of that book is: "Look, Tabitha's building is on fire, and her mother needs rescuing." I'll have students who are in book 3. That book starts with: "Let's get a new dog." These students have all been given the same tools, yet they use them differently. Help me, Lord, to sharpen the tools of my struggling craftspeople. Help them to have comprehension.

# JUST YOU AND ME, KID

*So we rebuilt the wall till*
*all of it reached half its height,*
*for the people worked with all their heart.*

NEHEMIAH 4:6

Lord, today I sit with a student in a study room off the main library. In her regular class, I have been told, she is busy entertaining others and making sure she's noticed. These traits have put her well behind her peers. Her parents have contacted me for private tutoring. Alone, she is a joy. Alone, she doesn't need to entertain. Alone, she knows that I notice her every move. Today we're working on her reading. Two grade levels behind, she's afraid that reading is impossible. Alone, it is. Together, we can conquer. Together, we find books at a level she understands and about topics that interest her. Together, we hold a bookmark under the sentence she needs to read. And, together, we celebrate each small step. Thank You, Lord, for each small step.

# NEWFANGLED IDEAS

*For lack of guidance a nation falls,*
*but many advisers make victory sure.*

PROVERBS 11:14

Teachers will try anything to help students comprehend, Father. And, Lord, I thank You that so often master teachers share with those of us who feel clueless. I heard some advice the other day that I'm going to try. The advice: light green ink. I was somewhat taken aback. After all, I was raised in the "grade in red ink" era. The theory behind light green ink is: It's hard to see; students will really have to concentrate. True. And if they concentrate, that means they'll be leaning forward, mouthing the words, holding their fingers to the comments, and striving to understand our words. If they strive to understand, they are most likely to comprehend. I'm going to try it this semester, Lord. Thank You so much for the guiding advice of others.

# RUNNING IN THE HALL ALLOWED, THIS ONCE

*My purpose is. . .*
*so that they may have the full riches of*
*complete understanding, in order that they may*
*know the mystery of God, namely, Christ.*

COLOSSIANS 2:2

First thing in the morning, my young students get their lined paper and newly sharpened pencils, and their job is to copy a paragraph in good handwriting. The main reason for this is that I want them to read and comprehend what they're writing. Sometimes I write, "When you're finished, you may walk to the second-grade classroom and get the prize I've taped under the teacher's desk." I love the look on the face of the student who grasps the instructions. I love the surprise on the faces of the other students when they see him stand up and, seemingly without permission, waltz out of the room. And, most of the all, I love how for the rest of the week, all the students strive to comprehend. Lord, You offer a prize for those followers who strive to comprehend and follow Your words. Help me, Lord, to tackle this quest with the same thoroughness as these first graders.

# TWO BY TWO

*Two are better than one,*
*because they have a good return for their work.*

ECCLESIASTES 4:9

Throughout my years of teaching, Lord, I have been blessed to encounter many wonderful parents. Their example makes me yearn for the days when I hold my own child. I pray that I remember the fine parenting skills displayed by these special mothers and fathers. I think about fathers especially—and I look at my husband and anticipate wondrous things from him. I want him to share in every aspect of raising our child. That means I hope he'll attend the parent/teacher conferences with me. My memories of parent/teacher conferences are an array of mothers and me. For some reason, the parent/teacher conference has the reputation of belonging to the moms. It's not true. When I sit across from two parents, both working toward a common goal—successful parenting—I want to shout with joy. And fathers ask different questions than mothers. Mothers focus on nurturing; fathers focus on facts. Thank You, Lord, for parents—fathers especially.

# TIME MANAGEMENT

*In [Christ] are hidden all the treasures*
*of wisdom and knowledge.*

COLOSSIANS 2:3

Lord, ten-minute time slots are allotted for parent/teacher conference day. Some appointments will only take two minutes! There's only so many ways to tell parents, "Your child is doing great!" Ten minutes is only perfect for the students who are at grade level. "Look, here's what she's doing successfully. Here are areas that need work." I try to work it so that parents who need more time get more time. "Your child is struggling" is a message that cannot be accomplished in ten minutes. Examples need to be displayed. Explanations need to be given. Questions need to be asked. Suggestions need to flow. Lord, during this last type of conference, my wisdom and knowledge seem to decrease—probably because I'm so distressed that one of my flock is floundering. It is so hard to be the bearer of unwanted news. Help me, Lord, to speak the truth in a manner pleasing to You. Help me look for ways to help the students, the parents, and myself. Stay beside the struggling children and lift them up.

# The Counsel of Many

*Serve wholeheartedly,*
*as if you were serving the Lord, not men.*

Ephesians 6:7

A conference can be between a few or many, Father, and I wonder what it was like to sit with the apostles and confer. I wonder what it was like to have such a skilled and fair leader as Jesus in the midst. What a team they must have been. I am thankful that, like Jesus, I am surrounded by many skilled and wise team members. They're called teachers and administrators. They are shepherds, and, Lord, what a blessing that I am counted in their number. Help us, Lord, to confer like the apostles and to do Your will by serving children.

# BIND US TOGETHER, LORD

*Because when the plowman plows*
*and the thresher threshes,*
*they ought to do so in the hope of*
*sharing in the harvest.*

1 CORINTHIANS 9:10

I've attended many instructional conferences, Lord. I've been both onstage (with hundreds of eyes looking at just me) and in the audience (my eyes, along with hundreds of others, looking at some other brave soul). My favorite moment, when I'm attending a conference, is just before it begins. I scan the program and choose the workshops I want to attend. Some of my best classroom endeavors have been the ideas of others. My favorite moment, when I'm speaking at a conference, is when I walk offstage. Thank You, Lord, for the courage to get in front of crowds. And, thank You for the courage of others to do the same.

# An Apple for the Teacher

*Whatever you do,*
*work at it with all your heart,*
*as working for the Lord, not for men.*

COLOSSIANS 3:23

Lord, You know I never planned on becoming a teacher. I earned a degree in journalism. I wanted to write interesting stories for *Reader's Digest*. Instead, after college, I waited tables. A few years later, I was offered a job teaching at a Christian school. Waitressing meant cash in the pocket and sleeping late in the morning. Teaching elementary school meant early mornings and slim paychecks twice a month. My parents were thrilled. My friends were enthusiastic. *Job security,* they claimed. Looking back, I realize that my decision to leave the restaurant field and enter the teaching field has shaped me into who I am today, and I am thankful that I made the right decision. Thank You, Lord, for Your guidance. Thank You for opportunities. Thank You for taking care of me.

# SHOULD I STAY OR SHOULD I GO?

*All a man's ways seem right to him,*
*but the LORD weighs the heart.*
*To do what is right and just*
*is more acceptable to the LORD than sacrifice.*

PROVERBS 21:2–3

Lord, I'm standing here looking at the accumulation of fourteen years. Yes, fourteen years. I have notes from parents of students long graduated. I have photos of field trips to sites no longer in existence. I even still own a student workbook for using a library's card catalogue. I'm getting married in a few months, and up to this point, I've taught elementary school during the day and college in the evening. Many of my friends do the same. Lord, I'm leaving the elementary work setting. No more notes from parents (at least I hope). No more field trips herding more than a hundred kids. And now the students will know more about the technology the library offers than I do. Lord, let the decisions we make about who and where to teach be guided by You.

# THE QUEEN OF DENIAL

*And the wise heart will know*
*the proper time and procedure.*
*For there is a proper time and*
*procedure for every matter.*

ECCLESIASTES 8:5–6

Father, I want to ask You for guidance as we make decisions about a student's future. Seldom am I torn about sending a child to the next grade level. Most students are ready to proceed. Some years, *all* are ready to proceed. I thank You for those years. But then it happens—what every teacher dreads—possible retention. We no longer call it "holding back." We call it "placing a child in the appropriate grade." If a child is truly failing, I lose sleep over the sorrow of it all, but I do not agonize over the decision. Lord, I want Your guidance with the child who is borderline. . .the child who needs more time. Give us—both parents and teachers—the wisdom to make the decision best for the child.

# I GET THE FRONT SEAT!

*Calling the Twelve to him,*
*he sent them out two by two.*

MARK 6:7

Lord, in a school setting, what looks to be a simple decision can actually be a time-consuming one. For example—deciding how to divide students into small groups on a field trip (what car they'll ride in and under which parent's supervision they'll fall). Best friends always want to ride together. It's not a good idea to give a single parent all the rowdy students. And it's always fair to make sure kids get a turn riding in the car of a beloved parent. I don't think I've ever once sat down, organized the travel for my field trip, and then managed to use the itinerary when the day finally arrived. Lord, help me to make the best decisions so our adventures are full of fun *and* safety. Most of all, Lord, help me be fair.

# TECHNICAL FOUL

*But in keeping with his promise
we are looking forward to
a new heaven and a new earth,
the home of righteousness.*

2 PETER 3:13

Lord, my husband and I are in the nosebleed section. The hockey game begins, and immediately two players are fighting and sent to time-out. My husband leans forward; this is entertainment! Me, I'm transported to my elementary classrooms and the many time-outs I've assigned. The men sitting out are not sorry for their offenses. Neither were some of my students. But You promise to forgive my sins if I follow Your teachings, and so often, Lord, I deserve time-outs. It's so amazing how the lessons of the classroom are demonstrated in adult life. I thank You for these moments that take me back in time and make me smile. I've had so many wonderful years as a teacher. I look forward to many more.

# HAPPY, HAPPY HOME

*"Turn the hearts of the fathers
to their children and the disobedient to
the wisdom of the righteous—
to make ready a people
prepared for the Lord."*

LUKE 1:17

I'm sitting here with report cards in front of me, Father. There's a whole section designed for me to write comments. My favorite comments are: "Doing great!" "Top of the class!" "A joy to teach." My least favorite comments are: "Behavior hinders learning." "Bothers fellow students." "Is unable to listen." As I strive to come up with the right words, I'm struck by how many different parenting styles are exampled in my classroom. I refer to them as the "Goldilocks Methods." Some parents are too strict. Some parents are too easy. And some parents are just right. But You know, Lord, my kids with behavior problems come from varying methods of parenting. Lord, I pray for these parents who are doing the best they can. Help them, Lord, to model a way of life that follows Your teachings. Let the "just right" be tailored for every child.

# GREAT EXPECTATIONS

*No discipline seems pleasant at the time,
but painful.
Later on, however, it produces a harvest of
righteousness and peace for those who
have been trained by it.*

HEBREWS 12:11

Father, it used to be that if a child got in trouble at school, he'd go home and get in trouble all over again. In most cases, that's no longer true. Lord, I want to thank You for the parents who expect a certain level of behavior from their children. I want to thank You for the parents who not only expect *but* who have also taught their children the rudiments of social structure. I want to thank the parents who believe that throughout the school year, discipline is a triangle involving parents, teacher, and child. I want to thank the children who try—and trying is all we can truly expect—to do right.

# TEACH ME TO WAIT

*. . .a spirit of power,*
*of love and of self-discipline.*

2 TIMOTHY 1:7

Lord, discipline can be quite good—self-discipline, that is. I recall a study that was done with marshmallows. Two marshmallows were put on a plate, and an elementary school child was put in the room with the marshmallows and told, "If you want, you can eat the marshmallows now, but if you wait until I come back, you'll get the whole bag of marshmallows." Of course, some children ate the marshmallows immediately. Others tried to wait but couldn't. And a few didn't eat the marshmallows. They sang, skipped, or hummed, trying to keep their minds off the marshmallows. Scientists followed the academic careers of those students and discovered that the students who were able to wait for gratification outperformed those who needed instant gratification.

Lord, like those children who couldn't wait, I tend to want everything now. I want spelling words memorized, multiplication tables learned, and comprehension high. Help me to know when "now" is not the time.

# THE END OF THE DAY

*He will not let your foot slip—*
*he who watches over you will not slumber.*

PSALM 121:3

Years ago, I sat down in a comfy chair and delved into a piece of fiction. The heroine of the story was a teacher. In the book, the author had the dismissal bell ring, and the kindergarten teacher looked up from scooping seeds out of a pumpkin and dismissed her class. I dropped that book. Father, I'm often amazed at how society views school teaching. They see it as an eight-to-three, easy job. I don't know any teachers who simply dismiss their class. I walk my students out, because even though the Holy Spirit walks beside them, many of them have notes in their folders that command: "Do not let (insert name) pick my child up." As I stand in our assigned sidewalk square, I busily keep note of where each child is and who is picking up that child. I hear that many, many years ago, students freely left the school building to climb into buses or cars or to walk home alone. I pray, Lord, that my own children may experience that type of freedom.

# GOOD-BYE

*Sons are a heritage from the LORD,*
*children a reward from him.*
*Like arrows in the hands of a warrior*
*are sons born in one's youth.*
*Blessed is the man whose quiver is full of them.*

PSALM 127:3–5

Father, when I open the doors after the final bell, there's a sea of cars outside. They contain families picking up children. Some moms and dads park, leave the car, and wait on the sidewalk. Others wait in the car, and the sixth-grade helpers walk the younger students out to the car. Often we see past students, now old enough to drive, who actually "want" to pick up their siblings—to show off both their age and their car. Lord, I thank You that when I open the doors after the final bell, there's a sea of cars containing families picking up children.

# No Running in the Hall

*" 'I will punish you as your deeds deserve,*
*declares the LORD.' "*

JEREMIAH 21:14

He fidgets in his seat, a restless soul. I don't think he's sorry he was running in the hall, but I do believe he's sorry he got caught. It's my job to watch the clock for ten minutes. That's the cost of getting caught running in the hall. He's miserable, Lord. He can hear the shouts of the other students. He just knows he's missing something important. He looks at me, then he looks at the clock. *Why aren't the hands moving?* Finally, I say, "You're free." He pops up and heads for the door, only to pause. Quickly he heads back in and gives me a hug. Oh, Father, thank You for these children and the opportunity to help them on their path to adulthood.

# It's Raining, It's Pouring

*"I have set my rainbow in the clouds,*
*and it will be the sign of the covenant*
*between me and the earth."*

GENESIS 9:13

The rain pours down as the three o'clock bell sounds, Lord. Another teacher and I borrow umbrellas and head outside. It's our duty to herd the students through puddles to their cars. Cold is creeping up my shoes and settling on my nylons. My nose is starting to run. I hold the umbrella in one hand, a child in the other. Siblings follow, purposely trudging through the puddles. Then we see it. The rainbow. Lord, You made a promise. You would never again destroy the world by flood. Just the sight of that rainbow stills my shivers. The children *ooh* and *aah*. Thank You for rainy days that help me remember Your promises.

Duties

# SPIT-SHINED

*They washed whenever they entered
the Tent of Meeting or approached the altar,
as the LORD commanded Moses.*

EXODUS 40:32

Lord, every Monday my students pick their job for the week. Many love Line Leader. (There's a thrill in being first.) Others want Errand Person. (Freedom!) Teacher's Helper is popular. (Passing out papers is a real draw.) The duty always picked last is Clean-up Person. I don't blame my students. It's my least favorite job, too, especially when I am helping in the church kitchen after a potluck. Still, there are the rare individuals who actually like being Clean-up Person. This child of Yours cringes that I allow chalk dust to collect in the eraser tray. This child doesn't allow glue to spill over from a paper to a desk. This child never leaves a sandwich in a lunch box overnight. I love this child of Yours and long to share his habits. Thank You, Lord, for this individual who makes me more aware of how precious my environment is and how important it is that I take care of it.

# PASS THE PEPPERONI

*"Never again will they hunger;*
*never again will they thirst.*
*The sun will not beat upon them,*
*nor any scorching heat."*

REVELATION 7:16

My least favorite duty, Father, is "lunchroom," when I have to walk around the cafeteria granting students restroom privileges, opening stubborn juice cartons, reminding students to go get napkins, and encouraging them to eat. Some students dig right in, and twenty seconds after they sit down, they're finished. Others eat at a normal speed. And others are simply not hungry, ever—unless it's pizza day. My main job is to make sure the students eat at least something. "Three bites," I urge one. "Ummm, I love ham sandwiches," I inform another. And I stop yet another child from sharing *all* his food with all his classmates. When they leave, the floor is awash with potato chips, used napkins, and straws. In America, we have an abundance of food. These students have never been hungry. Neither have I. Lord, help them learn to appreciate Your bounty. Help me to appreciate it, too.

# DETENTION

*We must pay more careful attention,*
*therefore, to what we have heard,*
*so that we do not drift away.*

HEBREWS 2:1

They come into my room with their lists, Lord. Some are writing one hundred times: *I will not. . .* Others are copying down two pages of behavior rules. Some will just put their heads down. It's my week for detention duty, and late each afternoon, I'm stuck in my room watching over the unruly. I feel as unruly as they do, Father. I cannot leave my desk. I am a guard. Some of the children are often in detention. The punishment means nothing to them. Others are distressed and will change their ways. Some have no clue why they're here. Lord, the next time these children face a behavior choice, let them choose to follow Your example.

# NEED SOAP?

*Do your best to present yourself to God as one approved,*
*a workman who does not need to be ashamed and who*
*correctly handles the word of truth.*

2 TIMOTHY 2:15

Lord, I am too accepting. I no longer flinch at bad words. I seldom close my eyes at sultry scenes on television. And although I shake my head at the way many teenagers dress, I no longer feel the urge to chase them down and offer them a really big sweater. It took a young child—and the movie *E. T.*—to show me the error of my ways. The characters were dressed fine. There were no sultry scenes. But every time a bad word was uttered, I watched that first grader flinch, and I was ashamed *because I didn't*. As the adult, I'm supposed to be a guardian. I failed, Lord. Please help me to do a better job.

# DEAR DAUGHTER

*If it is encouraging, let him encourage,*
*if it is contributing to the needs of others,*
*let him give generously;*
*if it is leadership, let him govern diligently;*
*if it is showing mercy, let him do it cheerfully.*

ROMANS 12:8

"You can do it!" "Have a good day!" "I love you!" "We're proud of you!" "You are beautiful!" Lord, one year I had a student who really looked forward to lunchtime. When the bell rang, she would smile and get her lunch box. We'd traipse down to the cafeteria, and after sitting down, she'd reach into her sandwich bag and pull out a napkin. Her mother always wrote encouraging messages on the napkins. I'd read them aloud to the class. We really looked forward to our message of the day. I still have some of these napkins in my scrapbook. Often, if the afternoon didn't progress perfectly for a classmate, the little girl gave away her napkins so someone else would be cheered. What a way to spread the message. Thank You, Lord, for encouraging moments like these.

# A HAPPY HEART

*One of them, when he saw he was healed,*
*came back, praising God in a loud voice.*
*He threw himself at Jesus' feet and thanked him—*
*and he was a Samaritan.*

LUKE 17:15–16

Lord, I just opened my e-mail and saw that I had a message. My heart sank. It's only the second week. Surely there can be no questions. I've not even assigned homework yet. I click on my message and see a name from last semester. I feel a smile coming on. I open the e-mail and read the message from a student who successfully completed my English 101 class and is now taking English 102. "Thank you," she wrote. "I feel so prepared." Oh, Lord, her message made my day. Maybe I *am* meant to be a teacher. Thank You, Lord, for making students who say "thank you." And, Lord, help me to deserve thank-yous from more students.

# THE GRAND PRIZE

*I press on toward the goal
to win the prize for which God
has called me heavenward in Christ Jesus.*

PHILIPPIANS 3:14

Nebraska—*Lincoln!* Arizona—*Phoenix!* Texas—*Austin!* A third-grade boy's knowledge of state capitals has brought the classroom to its knees, Father. No one can beat him, not even me. We've had the most fun! Some teachers cringe if they are shown up by a student. I think it's great, as long as the student doesn't gloat. And, in third grade, it makes the other students work harder because maybe, *just maybe,* they can find out what they do better than I. Lord, I thank You for these students who learn for learning's sake and enjoy the "game" aspect more than the competition. Help me to mimic their quest for knowledge and find more avenues to encourage full attention.

# WELL DONE

*Therefore encourage each other with these words.*

1 THESSALONIANS 4:18

"There are teachers all around us. . .it's our willingness to learn from them that makes the difference." I don't know who said it, Father, but I read it today, and it made me glad. Lord, every once in a while, I need a reminder—a reminder that I'm not alone. Thank You for quotes and proverbs and praise. Thank You for Your Word that uplifts me.

# I Take My Pen in Hand

*Jesus did many other things as well.*
*If every one of them were written down,*
*I suppose that even the whole world would not have*
*room for the books that would be written.*

John 21:25

When I taught elementary school, I learned family secrets via the students' attempts at writing. Thankfully, most were unique fabrications. Kindergartners wrote of pizza-glutted Thanksgiving feasts. Third graders claimed their parents (always so much younger than I) were seventy years old or more. Sixth graders were willing to share the dreaded secret of who smoked in the family. College is a whole new influx of information, and how I wish I could consider it fabricated. While reading freshman comp papers, I've illegally crossed the border, partied until I passed out, been in lethal car accidents, and lost boyfriends. Thankfully, I've also read of family reunions, births, and finding You. Words paint a vivid picture on the pages of our children's lives. Lord, help me to remember to pray for my students and their future chapters. How I wish I knew the stories of their lives all had happy endings.

# SECOND CHANCES

*Be wise in the way you act toward outsiders;*
*make the most of every opportunity.*

COLOSSIANS 4:5

For their first essay, I offer the freshmen class a gift. I take their papers home and make comments (think word choice, parallelism, format, and grammar advice). I hand the papers back, and they have the opportunity to rewrite. The majority of students appreciate the practice, learn from the experience, and want me to do it for every paper. The first year I did this, I didn't make the students staple the original I'd bled on (the ol' red-pen treatment) to the back of their revised copy. It didn't take long before I realized I was grading some of the originals again. Now the students have to staple. This inspires more of them to take the time to actually look at my comments and attempt to make changes. But a few still staple my comments to the back of a newly printed original. Father, how often do You give us second chances that we ignore? Help us to recognize the gifts and opportunities You give us. Help us to take advantage of them and, by doing so, appreciate You more.

# Confinements

*I wait for your salvation, O LORD,*
*and I follow your commands.*

PSALM 119:166

I hand out the writing assignment sheet, and the students peruse the stipulations. Some see the 500-word-count and cringe. How will they ever come up with *that* many words? Others shrug. No problem. They can find that many words in their sleep, and making things fit is an ingrained habit. Others gnaw on their bottom lips in concern. How will they ever tell their story in so *few* words? When the papers are turned in, the majority of students manage to make their papers fit the assignment. A few papers have words that spill over into the 550s, 600s, and even 700s. These students believe their words are so wonderful that I won't mind that they ignored the word count. Other students try to change their font size and adjust the margins. These students believe I'm so blind that I won't notice they only wrote 300 words. Lord, You've given us stipulations in the Bible. And, like my students, Your followers cross the line or fall short, but sometimes they manage to get it right. Thank You, Lord, for giving us the Bible, which tells us what to do. Help us to be like the students with ingrained habits instead of like the students who believe their way is all right no matter how far they stray from the assignment.

# A LAST-DITCH EFFORT

*"There is nothing concealed that will not be disclosed,*
*or hidden that will not be made known."*

MATTHEW 10:26

They turn their papers in on Tuesday, Lord. I remind them to staple their rough draft to the back. Now I have a stack of essays to occupy my weekend and evenings for a week. At home and in my office, I grade. On Thursday, a young lady hands me a paper and says, "It's my rough draft. I forgot to staple it to the back." I stick it in my folder and forget about it. At home and in my office, I continue grading. I have seventy-five college freshmen. Each paper takes an average of ten minutes of my time. Finally, I finish and add the percentages to my grade book. Then I note the names of the students who did not turn in papers, and one gives me pause. It's the young lady who gave me her rough draft late. Getting out my class folder, I find the paper. She did turn in the rough draft, but stapled behind it is her paper. In college, the rule is no late papers. She tried to sneak one in. Lord, how often do we hope You won't notice when we break Your rules? I write the student a note. She's caught, just like I'm so often caught. Help us all work harder to reach our goal.

# THE WATCHER

*Obey your leaders and submit to their authority.*
*They keep watch over you as men*
*who must give an account.*
*Obey them so that their work will be a joy,*
*not a burden,*
*for that would be of no advantage to you.*

HEBREWS 13:17

He walks in and sits in the back of the class, Father. He's my boss, and it's his job to evaluate my teaching ability. What better way than to attend an actual class? The students all notice, especially the young lady whom he sits near. I joke and tell her to be nice to him—offer him chocolate, help him keep up with the class. . . . Then I begin. The lesson is subjects and verbs—not a topic you'll see on a Monday night Lifetime movie. He begins taking notes. Because I'm nervous, I'm spewing out words faster than a runaway train—trying to make a ho-hum lesson a little bit inviting. He writes quickly. The students are keeping up. What a relief. They answer questions. I set them to work and walk around. For one activity, I send a student to the front and have her teach the class. Is that a smile on his face? Lord, You are foremost in my world; and, yes, You evaluate me. Help me, Father, to set an example outside my classroom as well as in it. Oh, Father, I'd like to think that occasionally (dare I think often?) You have a smile on Your face as You watch me.

## THE LISTENER

*"Stop judging by mere appearances,*
*and make a right judgment."*

JOHN 7:24

Lord, I take my class to the library. It's been arranged for weeks. The librarian graciously gives his time to discuss databases, on-line research, and interlibrary loan. I've arranged for a thirty-minute session. The librarian gets so involved in his presentation that he takes fifty minutes. The second half of my lesson is now null and void, so I settle back and listen to the librarian. I've adjusted my calendar before; I'll do it again. When he finishes, he passes out evaluations. Not only are my students to assess him, but so am I. Personally, I don't like evaluations. The students, anxious to leave, breeze through the papers. A few take their time—but are they evaluating his knowledge or their own personal interest in coming to the library to learn? I slip the evaluation in my briefcase. I am uncomfortable evaluating him. How can I evaluate him fairly? I've brought my students to the library too many times. I know the presentation backward and forward. I graded papers during his lesson. I cannot evaluate him, Lord. I wasn't even listening. I wonder how many times the critiques of an audience are taken as fact when, in truth, the audience wasn't paying attention. Help me, Lord, to be careful with the words I use to assess others.

# THE SUGGESTION

*" 'Well done, good and faithful servant!' "*

MATTHEW 25:21

It's evaluation time, Lord. The seasoned professional enters the room, sits in the back, and takes out the evaluation form. That form usually contains a place to offer suggestions. Evaluators are usually teachers themselves. They've stood in front of classrooms for years, saying, "Never leave a space blank." Sometimes we take this suggestion too far. I heard a seasoned instructor lament about what to put in the suggestion spot. Apparently, the new hire she'd been evaluating had done a superb job. I've seen some evaluations with advice in the suggestion box that bordered on ridiculous. But at least the space wasn't left blank! Lord, sometimes the last words should simply be, "Well done." Help me to remember that.

# SOMEBODY'S WATCHING

*"The LORD will watch over your coming
and going both now and forevermore."*

PSALM 121:8

I've sat through many evaluations, Lord. The first came when, as a child, teachers evaluated me on a form called the report card. My parents then went home and evaluated the report card, which resulted in a parent evaluation called a family discussion. Those evaluations plagued me from kindergarten through college graduation. Most were just, whether I wanted to admit it or not. As a waitress, my managers evaluated me. Most commented on my dependability but wished I would ease up on my bossiness. Yes, there's one of my flaws—a flaw common mostly in children—I'm bossy. When I became an elementary schoolteacher, my principals were so overworked that in fourteen years, I think maybe I got evaluated only three or four times. The college scene doesn't have a shortage of evaluators. A chair can evaluate; so can a dean; and in a pinch, a seasoned professor fills in. I get evaluated often. And I've actually made some positive changes from the criticisms, er. . .I believe the politically correct term is *suggestions*. Lord, be with the people who evaluate me and be with the people whom I evaluate. Help *just* to be the operative word. Lord, I thank You for watching over me.

# MICKEY D'S

*Follow my example,*
*as I follow the example of Christ.*

1 CORINTHIANS 11:1

The first few years I taught at a small, private school, Lord, we didn't have a library. Once a month I loaded my kindergartners into cars, and off we went to the public library. They loved it; but what they loved even more was our trip to McDonald's afterward. Happy Meals were handed out, and my classes took over a whole section of the restaurant. We prayed, we ate, and then we cleaned up after ourselves. Often, after we ventured to the play area, I watched as a McDonald's employee headed over to our spot with a broom and dustpan. I watched as relief washed over her face. She expected smashed fries on the floor, smeared ketchup on the tables, and trash galore. Lord, help us always to remember that others watch us pray, recognize we're Christians, and then have to clean up after us.

# FIRST IN LINE

*"But many who are first will be last,
and the last first."*

MARK 10:31

Father, the local community college is hosting a Readfest. My third graders travel from booth to booth. They listen to stories, fish for prizes, and get autographs from the students dressed up as storybook characters (Snoopy seems to be the favorite). Taking our place in line at one booth, we wait our turn. Suddenly, a barrage of children accosts us, cutting in line, and basically taking over from the students who were first. I gather my class around me more concerned about safety than anything else. Finally, a teacher shows up. She smiles at me and says, "Sorry," before joining her students in the prime spots they, in essence, stole. Lord, please help me to be an active leader and not a passive leader. Please help me to teach politeness and consideration, instead of to the victor go the spoils.

# DELIVERY GUARANTEED

*Because of this oath,*
*Jesus has become the guarantee of a better covenant.*

HEBREWS 7:22

You know there are examples in the book, Lord. In class, I pass out examples. On review day, I put examples on the overhead. And, sometimes, Lord, by test time, the students grasp the concept. *Sometimes.* Other times, I have students coming to me with homework in hand and the words "I don't understand" on their lips. After the test, I hear the words "I thought I understood." Each year, I discard old examples for new, always looking for examples that will guarantee understanding. But there are no guarantees. What works for Dick doesn't work for Jane. When Jane fumbles, Dick takes off. Lord, thank You for Your example. Thank You for the Bible that encourages understanding. Thank You for Your guarantee that heaven is obtainable.

# CALL ON ME

*Our desire is not that others might be relieved while you*
*are hard pressed, but that there might be equality.*

2 CORINTHIANS 8:13

I travel to a nearby college for a curriculum meeting, Father, and I am the only one from my school attending. I feel inadequate for the task; I am the new kid on the block, and I keep waiting for someone to stand up, point at me, and yell, "Fraud!" I park my car and journey through an unknown campus. Soon I'm in a room with my peers, only I feel inadequate. Surely I'm the only English professor in the room who once mispronounced *cicadas* in front of a class. Surely I'm the only English professor who occasionally writes a sentence that includes a misspelling on the board. Surely I'm the only English professor in the room who somehow loses my overheads between the office and the classroom. During the meeting, I tell myself to keep quiet, nod in agreement, and resist the cookie plate that is being passed around. Yet, as I nibble on a cookie, I find myself offering suggestions and contributing to a dialogue started by seasoned professionals. Lord, I ask that You guide me during the days when I feel inadequate for the task. I can grow only by accepting challenges. Thank You, Lord, for moments to grow.

# CALL ME GRANDPA

*"Rise in the presence of the aged,
show respect for the elderly and revere your God."*

LEVITICUS 19:32

"I'm the oldest in the class." The words are part wonder, part fear, and part acceptance, Lord. "No, you're not," I reply. "I am." In college, one of the beauties is the diversity of the crowd. My freshman class might have a sixteen-year-old in the back row and a sixty-year-old in the front row. The benefit, of course, are the examples set. After an hour of absorbing the sixteen-year-old's energy, the sixty-year-old almost skips out of the class. After an hour of listening to the sixty-year-old's wisdom, the sixteen-year-old makes an effort to eliminate slang from his classroom language. Lord, thank You for unique attributes that each student brings to the classroom.

# PASS THE PACIFIER

*Treat younger men as brothers.*

1 TIMOTHY 5:1

"I'm the youngest in the class." "Yes, you are," I reply. "Now, quit bragging." You see, the sixteen-year-old comes in with a fourth part—pride. I'm divided in my opinion about high school students stepping into my college freshman class. For the mature young lady who finally finds a place to belong, I say, "Welcome." To the young athlete whose eyes close (football practice takes up a lot of time) during my class, I say, "Enjoy your high school years; they are like no others." To the young man who has senioritis, I say, "Why are you here? It will mean so much more when the time is right." To the driven young man who has all his goals in sight, I say, "I wish I had half your dedication." But it's not up to me to judge who stays and who goes. And when the semester is over, sometimes it's the student with senioritis who surprises me the most. Lord, thank You again for unique attributes that each student brings to the classroom.

# STILL WAITING

*Yet the LORD longs to be gracious to you;*
*he rises to show you compassion.*
*For the LORD is a God of justice.*
*Blessed are all who wait for him!*

ISAIAH 30:18

"I'm the slowest in the class." "It's not always quantity," I reply. "Sometimes it's quality." And often I'm telling the truth. The first person to turn in a test seldom receives the highest score. The last person to turn in a test usually has a better chance. For all that, who wants to finish last? We all respect that first person. *What do they know that we don't?* we wonder. The problem is, slowness has two definitions. One has to do with time, and the other has to do with ability. Father, both qualities require effort and prayer. Both need the compassion of an understanding environment. I sometimes get impatient with my slow students. Help me to remember and praise You, Lord, for the unique abilities of each student.

# TOP OF THE CLASS

*"Where is the wise man?*
*Where is the scholar?*
*Where is the philosopher of this age?"*

1 CORINTHIANS 1:20

"I'm the smartest person in the class." I never reply, Lord; I'm afraid of what I might say. Since the first gathering of children in a classroom environment, not only have teachers been categorizing students; students have been categorizing themselves. The smartest in the class comes with his own set of fears, and sometimes as a teacher I'm more at a loss as to how to help this student than any other. Lord, thank You for each student in the classroom. Help me, Lord, to know how to guide them.

# COMMUNICATION

*A friend loves at all times.*

PROVERBS 17:17

Lord, one year I had the son of a good friend as a student. What a year that was. I doubt if any mother was ever as informed as my friend the year I taught her son. Every day she heard praises or suggestions. Her son was *extremely* well behaved because he knew that I spoke with his mother every night. And, of course, he knew that often he was the topic of conversation. Father, wouldn't it be grand if all parents had that kind of inside track with a child's teacher? Teaching my friend's child could have meant the end of a friendship, but we'd built up such a level of trust—my friend and I—that communication was uncensored. Thank You, Lord, for friendships that allow for change.

# BREAKING THE ICE

*Jonathan said to David,*
*"Whatever you want me to do,*
*I'll do for you."*

1 SAMUEL 20:4

---

"Why doesn't my child have any friends?" I've been asked this question more than once, Lord, and it's not an easy one to answer. Some children are loners due to extreme shyness. Others simply don't know how to be friends. And others don't know how to keep friends. Teachers are very aware of the friendships in the classroom—some of which are beautiful to behold. I've seen friendships last from childhood to marriage. But every teacher's heart sinks when a little one is unable to find his or her niche. Lord, I know how much friendship means to me. Please help these little ones to find their place in life and to find strong friends—true friends, like David and Jonathan—to journey with them.

# MAKE NEW FRIENDS, BUT KEEP THE OLD

*"My command is this:*
*Love each other as I have loved you."*

JOHN 15:12

Lord, I love watching the children walk into the kindergarten classroom. The potential for acceptance—for friendship—will never be this expansive again. The children's eyes sweep the classroom, and the thought is: *Who will be my friend?* There are no boy/girl boundaries. There are no more-toys/less-toys boundaries. Popularity is open to all. In a class of five-year-olds, whoever is willing to give a tap on the head during a game of Duck, Duck, Goose is qualified to be a friend. I wish this ease of acceptance could continue through the upper grades.

# ONE IS SILVER, AND THE OTHER GOLD

*"This is my command:*
*Love each other."*

JOHN 15:17

There are two girls I've watched for years, Lord. They are cousins. One is a grade ahead of the other. Lord, I am envious of their friendship. It's not the kind that will end if they change schools or move to different states. It's the kind of friendship that will still be in place through marriages and children and when they are both in wheelchairs and waiting in line for the four o'clock special at the local buffet. In our mobile society, these two young ladies remind me of a time when generations stayed in one place. Lord, I wish I'd grown up with a close sister or relative like this. Watch over these young ladies, and help them to nurture the bond they are so fortunate to have.

# A Call for Action

*"But wisdom is proved right by her actions."*

MATTHEW 11:19

I've only had to call social services once, Lord. My fingers shook from the sorrow I felt. I finally got connected to the person I needed, stated my fears, and was told, "That's not abuse. It's neglect. We don't have the manpower to investigate." Frustration swelled up in my gut, and I hung up the phone feeling helpless. Lord, there are children out there who are not in loving homes. There are children who come to school, and it is their only safe haven. Lord, watch over those children. And give me the wisdom to know how to help. Let my frustration be followed by action.

# FINISHED PRODUCT

*"Where did this man get these things?"*
*they asked.*
*"What's this wisdom that has been given him,*
*that he even does miracles!*
*Isn't this the carpenter?"*

MARK 6:2–3

Lord, we've entered a museum housing exquisite works of art. My mouth is open in awe at the paintings displayed. My fingers itch to touch the sculptures. And where are my students? They are gathered around a tile setter who is replacing tile in one of the main hallways. I urge them forward, but they look back. He's mixing grout. He has a tool that swishes across the floor. He's crawling on his hands and knees.

Back at school, they write a paragraph about what they enjoyed the most about the museum. Not surprisingly, they liked watching the tile setter. Sometimes, Lord, learning takes an unexpected curve. Lord, remind me that creativity should not be restricted and that honest fascination should be encouraged.

# FOUR WALLS

*Then Philip ran up to the chariot*
*and heard the man reading Isaiah the prophet.*
*"Do you understand what you are reading?"*
*Philip asked. "How can I," he said,*
*"unless someone explains it to me?"*

ACTS 8:30–31

I teach an English 101 class in a room that's been around since before I was born. It has those chairs with the attached rounded, flat top that serves as a desk. I hated them as a student because I am not a size three. The air-conditioning unit for this room sounds like a groaning train. There's a whiteboard with another professor's notes still visible because he ignored the word "permanent" on the marker he used. The carpeting is dirt brown and has stains I do not want to identify. And most evenings students crowd in, hoping to improve their station in life. I've taught in this room for over five years, Father, and I am comfortable. So are the students.

Lord, Your followers taught in villages, tiny homes, chariots, and standing on rocks. I have electricity and overheads, and still I expect more. Help me to appreciate all I have.

# NOW WHERE DID I PUT IT?

*Be careful that you do not forget the LORD,*
*who brought you out of Egypt,*
*out of the land of slavery.*

DEUTERONOMY 6:12

Each of my elementary school children has a mailbox. I put graded papers, notes to parents, handouts from the office, and so on, in the mailboxes. At the end the day, the students are supposed to empty them. Yet I often look over to see that one of my charges has made it out of the classroom without his or her mail. Lord, these items are important. But, Lord, how many times have I forgotten important items? Watch over us, Lord. We are a forgetful people—look how often we've forgotten You.

# THE FINEST GIFTS HE BRINGS—
# PA-RUM-PA-PUM-PUM

*A gift opens the way for the giver*
*and ushers him into the presence of the great.*

PROVERBS 18:16

Lord, I'm decorating the Christmas tree. I've only been married a little over a year, so the ornaments from family are few and far between. But the ornaments from school are many and meaningful. On the top of my tree is an angel made for me by a mother who devoted so much time to helping in the classroom and cafeteria that she ought to have a building named after her. Look, here's a Play-Doh goose. This was given to me by my Brownie troop after we entered our homemade tree in a museum contest. There's a giant plastic-egg manger hanging from one limb. I've lost the Jesus baby that used to reside inside. Lord, I thank You for these tangible objects that Your children gave me. They are worth more than silver or gold because they are memories that soothe the heart.

# THE FINEST GIFTS
# HE BRINGS—PART TWO

*There is surely a future hope for you,*
*and your hope will not be cut off.*

PROVERBS 23:18

I could go on looking at the memories hanging as ornaments from my tree, but instead I'd rather think about the students. Some of them have kept in touch. Others have disappeared into the crevices of the United States. Maybe one day I'll turn on the television and see a past student delivering the news. Maybe one day I'll go into the neighborhood bank and a past student will authorize a loan. Maybe one day I'll enter the office of a doctor and there with a stethoscope will be first row, third seat. Thank You, Lord, for these gifts that hang from my tree and for offering these students, Your children, the greatest gift of all—a future with You.

# THE CHOSEN ONE

*Thanks be to God for his indescribable gift!*

2 CORINTHIANS 9:15

It's the Friday before the winter holiday. The students brought gifts, and now they sit in a circle as a holiday song plays. They each hold a present in their lap, count to three, and then pass the gift to the person to their left. They'll do this until the music stops.

Some simply enjoy the game. Others cannot wait to open whatever present they might wind up with. They tend to pass very quickly. A few have figured out which wrapped parcel they want. Through trial and error, they try to guess the moment I'll stop the music. Presents pile up at their feet. The students next to them glare empty-handed. Lord, help us to remember that it's not always the biggest and most gaily wrapped package that contains what we need most. Help us remember that Your Son, Jesus, born to a carpenter, is the greatest gift.

# PRECIOUS JEWELS

*May your father and mother be glad;*
*may she who gave you birth rejoice!*

PROVERBS 23:25

Spread across my desk is a clutter of gifts. Candles, flowers, perfume, and plaques that proclaim "World's Greatest Teacher" abound. It's the last day of school. In a matter of moments, the students were gone. They walked away holding the hand of the adult who will be their teacher for life. I am but a blink of an eye in their universe. I will gather the gifts and put them in a box to take home. Lord, I thank You for the moments You give me—moments to be a member of the village that raises a child. Let my village be ruled by You.

# Robbing Peter to Pay Paul

*Now finish the work,*
*so that your eager willingness to do it*
*may be matched by your completion of it,*
*according to your means.*

2 Corinthians 8:11

I am in my classroom from 8:30 a.m. until 3:00 p.m., Lord. That's six and a half hours. Once my students arrive, it takes ten minutes to settle in. I subtract thirty minutes for two recesses. Another twenty minutes for lunch. I subtract twenty minutes for chapel. I am left a fifty-minute elective. So, in all, I have the students for four hours and ten minutes. During that time I try to teach reading, math, science, history, language, spelling, and history. I can roughly spend thirty-five minutes a day on each subject. Thirty-five minutes! Okay, I have a few slow readers—can I borrow time from math? And what about restroom breaks? Show-and-tell? Lord, there is never enough time to get it all done. Help me find the time to do what should be done. Help me not leave anyone behind. Help me do it all with a cheerful heart.

## MODERN-DAY MOSES

*"May the LORD keep watch between you and me when we are away from each other."*

GENESIS 31:49

Another student just asked me if he can go inside for a drink of water, Lord. We have a fountain outside, but the water is warm. Inside, the water is cold—but I'm out here. If I send a student inside, there's no one to watch over him. Lord, sometimes we have to leave the safety of supervision in order to reap a better harvest. Some students will settle for the warm water because play is important to them. But some will brave the long, empty hallway. Thank You for watching over both kinds of wanderers—the safe and the daring.

# WHAT TO DO

*Not many of you should presume to be teachers,*
*my brothers, because you know that*
*we who teach will be judged more strictly.*

JAMES 3:1

Subbing for forty-five minutes in a Sunday school classroom should be a breeze after a week in a regular classroom. The third graders sit up when I enter the room. One boy, a stranger to me, ducks his head when it comes time to read aloud. The helper whispers, "He can't read." I'm appalled. Third grade! I'm ready to find his parents and rattle off a list of study skills they might try. "Don't," advised the regular teacher later. "They might not bring him back to class." Lord, I didn't offer my advice. I kept quiet, and it's haunted me ever since. Forgive me for not knowing what to do.

# READING GROUPS

*"But as for you,*
*be strong and do not give up,*
*for your work will be rewarded."*

2 CHRONICLES 15:7

Every teacher has her own method for holding reading groups. I use a chip method. I call my little group of five back to the reading table. In the center of the table, I place five chips. Each student reads a page. As long as they make no mistakes, the chips remain. If they make a mistake, a chip goes. It's very important to the students that *they* not be the one to cost the group a chip. There are flaws in this method, I agree. But I've had reading groups that lasted through recess. And the students are so proud of their successes! When the chips are gone, they know reading group—for that day—is over, but they also know tomorrow is another day. Lord, I thank You for successes. And for students who encourage each other when the chips are down.

# LEST WE FORGET

*So we make it our goal to please him,*
*whether we are home in the body*
*or away from it.*

2 CORINTHIANS 5:9

I have a whiteboard in my office. Right now I only have three items written on it. "Pray" is number one. I pray for my students. Number two is "Take Tuesday/Thursday syllabus to secretary." There's a line through that one because I did it last week. The third item is "Make February calendars." That goal has been on the board for a week. I need to do it today so I can hand them out on Wednesday. I always have to set visible goals now. I used to be able to remember everything in my mind. I'm not sure if my memory is failing because I'm getting older or because I have more to remember. Whatever it is, Lord, help me to never forget my first goal. Let me pray for students and classes alike.

# TEACH ME TO TEACH

*And the Lord's servant must not quarrel;*
*instead, he must be kind to everyone,*
*able to teach, not resentful.*

2 TIMOTHY 2:24

This New Year's, instead of making the "I'm Going to Lose Weight" goal, I made the "I'm Going to Be a Better Teacher" goal. I've already broken my goal, because yesterday when a student called me to find out what he missed in class, I told him to look at the syllabus. I should have taken five minutes and summarized what had taken place in the classroom. How many times, Lord, have I not given a simple five minutes? Lord, help me to slow down and think before I speak. Help me to be a better teacher.

# BE THERE

*I give you sound learning,*
*so do not forsake my teaching.*

PROVERBS 4:2

I once lost a college student simply because of my attendance policy. He missed more days than I allowed. I dropped him and felt guilt. I hated to think that because of a rigid policy, I discouraged a willing and able student. My goal is to retain students, not lose them! The next semester, I relaxed my policy. It was a bad idea. The students who "needed" to be there failed to attend because of lenient accountability. I lost more than one because they fell so far behind in classroom discussions and explanations that they couldn't catch up. My goal was not reached! I reinstated my attendance policy and no longer feel guilt. Lord, You have given us guidelines—policies—to follow, and when we fail to attend to them, we stumble and lose sight of the goal of reaching heaven. Help us, Lord, to understand Your Word and follow it.

# QUALITY NOT QUANTITY

*. . .turning your ear to wisdom*
*and applying your heart to understanding.*

PROVERBS 2:2

Lord, every semester twenty-five freshmen *enter* my English 101 class. Every semester I make a goal. Just this once, when the semester is over, twenty-five freshmen will *leave* my English 101 class. Some of my fellow instructors have retained every student from first day to last. I want a perfect semester, too! Lord, it has never happened. Some I lose the first week. They transfer to other classes or realize they were in the wrong class to begin with. As the semester toils on, I lose students to sickness, job changes, and, well, life just gets in the way. Lord, I made a goal that I had no control over. Help me to make reasonable goals. Help me to realize that the number doesn't matter as much as the teaching.

# TOSSING AND TURNING

*"So I strive always to keep
my conscience clear
before God and man."*

ACTS 24:16

I am often wrong, Lord. There, I've said it. I make mistakes. Mistakes that keep me awake at night. Mistakes that affect Your children. I sometimes think my biggest mistake is not relinquishing control to You. I play the blame game. It was my fault, the student's fault, the parent's fault, another teacher's fault, or the principal's fault. Truthfully, it is everybody's fault and nobody's. Mistakes happen. I need to remember that the best thing to do is listen carefully to what the other person has to say and try to come up with a solution that makes both parties happy. And if that doesn't work, let an arbitrator get involved. I think we're afraid of arbitrators, but isn't that somewhat what You are? I need to listen to You, God. I need to realize that if I'm bringing home a worry—then I need to let You guide me toward solving that worry for the good of the many, not the good of me.

# GOOD NIGHT, JOHN-BOY

*Consequently,*
*faith comes from hearing the message,*
*and the message is heard through*
*the word of Christ.*

ROMANS 10:17

Lord, as I walk down the hallway at the end of my day, all along the corridor, other instructors are still hard at work in their offices. They salute me with a chorus of good-byes. I hear them and respond, feeling a bit of what it might have felt like to grow up in a big, happy family—like on the television series *The Waltons. Good night, John-Boy. Goodnight, Mary Ellen. Good night, Grandpa.* What a blessed feeling it is to have a sense of belonging, of camaraderie. Lord, thank You for the sense of community that I find both at work and at church.

# RELAX

*Praise be to the God and Father*
*of our Lord Jesus Christ,*
*the Father of compassion*
*and the God of all comfort.*

2 CORINTHIANS 1:3

I'm tired, Lord. It's Wednesday night. I have papers to grade, a poster to create, phone calls to make, and I need to stop by the store and buy some flour for a project we're doing in class tomorrow. Will You notice if I'm not in church tonight? Is it really so important, this mid-week service? I'm feeling frantic; there's so much to do. Lord, every time I face this dilemma, skipping church is the *last* thing I should do. It's while I sit in the pew, listening to Your Word and fellow-shipping, that I feel the weight of the world leave my shoulders. Lord, You are my comforter. I always manage to get things done. And I'm happier when You are my first priority.

# ASLEEP AT THE WHEEL

*He said, "Go and tell this people:*
*'Be ever hearing, but never understanding;*
*be ever seeing, but never perceiving.' "*

ISAIAH 6:9

I can't believe it, Lord! Two students were trying to sleep in my 7:30 a.m. class! I'm indignant, disturbed, and puzzled. Schooling is so unimportant to them that they'd attempt (I kept waking them up) to fall asleep during a lecture. As I enter my office, my heart is beating quickly, and I am still coming up with ways to prevent it from happening tomorrow. I sit behind my desk and speculate. Soon I'm empathizing with my students. Lord, those students were *literally* sleeping, but how often am I *figuratively* sleeping when I should be hearing Your Word? I attend service, but when the sermon is over, I didn't hear a word. Lord, help me to be a better listener. Help my students, too. Let me present my lessons so they are informative *and* interesting.

# MADAM SECRETARY

*Whatever you do,*
*work at it with all your heart,*
*as working for the Lord,*
*not for men.*

COLOSSIANS 3:23

I've been extremely blessed, Lord! Every single school secretary I have worked with deserves double pay. Not because of how they have treated me, but because of how they treat everybody. They are the "right hand" of the principal or department chair. ("I need a memo sent out yesterday.") They are the instructor's "knight in shining armor." ("Here's the black construction paper you were looking for.") They are heroes to the students. ("Of course I have bandages." Or, "You'll find the math building just east of the library.") Thank You, Lord, for sending us these guiding angels.

# LEFTY

*"But when you give to the needy,*
*do not let your left hand know*
*what your right hand is doing."*

MATTHEW 6:3

I'd been working with the student for weeks, Lord. "Take the left lace. Tuck it over. . ." No matter what we did, we couldn't seem to create a bow that would tie her shoe. "Let's start again. This time take both shoestrings. . ." "Okay, now again. . ."

One day as we knelt side by side on the playground, one of my soccer boys tripped into us. "Oops, sorry, Teacher. Whatcha doing?" I didn't even get the chance to answer. With a glance, he took in the activity, knelt down, and said, "Here's how ya do it." Then, in a blink, he was gone. For the next few minutes, I watched that little girl tie her shoe over and over. She couldn't wait to get home to show her mom. You know, I should have introduced that left-handed soccer player to my left-handed shoe-tier weeks ago. Lord, help me to know when I am the chosen one and when You have someone else in mind.

# AUTOGRAPH PLEASE

*For no one has ever shown the mighty power*
*or performed the awesome deeds*
*that Moses did in the sight of all Israel.*

DEUTERONOMY 34:12

Lord, I'm worried about today's youth as I'm pretty sure my parents worried about my generation. They walk down the halls with the likenesses of movie stars and athletes on their folders. Lord, please help my students see past the glitter and glamour of Hollywood airbrushing and the NBA's million-dollar paychecks. Let them know the true heroes are in the Bible, in the church, and in their own homes.

# DADDY

*"I will be a Father to you,*
*and you will be my sons and daughters,*
*says the Lord Almighty."*

2 CORINTHIANS 6:18

He showed up thirty minutes early to pick up his son, Lord. I noticed him standing outside the door, patiently waiting. *Oh, no, no.* Within moments, I ushered him into the classroom and had him sitting in the back with a group of five little ones surrounding him. He held up addition flash cards and nodded at correct answers. Soon a little hand went to the man's knee. Another child scooted closer—I think just the scent of a father is different than the teacher or mother. Others in the class stole glances at the man who had entered their haven. Happiness seemed a tangible entity in my classroom. Lord, in a day when only the blessed have fathers, I thank You for this man who not only picks up his son early, but enters the classroom and models the glory of being a father.

# In the Blink of an Eye

*Go to the ant, you sluggard;*
*consider its ways and be wise!*

Proverbs 6:6

I'm not crazy about spiders, Lord, so when the daddy longlegs chose to visit my classroom one fine morning, I debated a few moments before granting him immunity from my foot. After all, he visited during my insect unit. I gathered my students around him and extolled his virtues. He's really not the most poisonous spider. He's just a gentle guy with a pill-like body, two eyes, and eight legs. He does not produce silk. A moment later, a fellow teacher popped in to see why my class was congested by the door. "Oh, a spider!" she exclaimed. And, knowing that I'm not crazy about spiders, she stepped on it for me. Since I did not know the life expectancy of a daddy longlegs, I had no closure for this lesson, and I urged the startled students to their seats. Lord, much like life, lessons do not always go as planned. Help us to adjust and do the best we can.

# I'M A TRAVELING MAN

*For you were like sheep going astray,*
*but now you have returned to the Shepherd*
*and Overseer of your souls.*

1 PETER 2:25

Lord, our class hamster often travels home with students for the weekend. He's quite the adventurer. One Monday he returned with a new gadget in his cage. All day we admired his new, boxlike climbing structure. What we didn't realize was that he could climb on top of this box, jump up, knock off the screen lid to his cage, and escape. It wasn't his escaping his cage that Monday evening that got us in trouble, Father. It was his interrupting the elders and deacons' meeting uninvited. Thankfully, Lord, they returned him to his rightful home, removed the new climbing structure, and left a note advising me to either secure the lid or get rid of the box. Lord, we often go to places we shouldn't. How thankful we are that You forgive us and help us to travel the right direction.

# THERE'S A BLUE ONE

*Now finish the work,*
*so that your eager willingness to do it*
*may be matched by your completion of it,*
*according to your means.*

2 CORINTHIANS 8:11

As we walk down the hall, Lord, a box of crayons tumbles to the floor. Without hesitating, the surrounding children hit their knees and start helping pick up the colorful array spread across the carpet. As a teacher, I want to say, "Keep walking. Let the owner pick them up." As a Christian, I need to notice the glory of watching children help others without needing encouragement to do so. I'm impatient, Lord. I want them where they're going when they're supposed to be there. Help me to recognize that not all interruptions are detrimental to my schedule. Help me to give when I need to.

# NEEDFUL THINGS

*Train the younger women. . .*
*to be self-controlled and pure,*
*to be busy at home, to be kind,*
*and to be subject to their husbands,*
*so that no one will malign the word of God.*

TITUS 2:4–5

I sit on the couch in my living room with a stack of papers to grade. I get comfortable and pull out the top paper. Here comes my husband. "Where's my green jacket?" We take care of that problem— he leaves. I get comfortable and pull out the top paper. The phone rings. It's my best friend, frazzled. She needs to talk. We take care of that problem. I get comfortable and pull out the top paper. The oven bell sounds. It's time to put dinner on the table. We take care of that. Later, my husband takes care of the dishes, and I get comfortable and pull out the top paper. The doorbell rings. Lord, I may not get the papers graded tonight, but thanks to good health and a willing spirit, I can set my alarm clock an hour early. Thank You for interruptions that prove just how much I'm needed by family and friends.

# GIDDY-UP

*So the word of God spread.*
*The number of disciples*
*in Jerusalem increased rapidly,*
*and a large number of priests*
*became obedient to the faith.*

ACTS 6:7

We pile into the van and head for Canyon de Chelley. It's a long weekend, Lord, and five of us—all teachers—are off on a journey. Our big adventure will be a horseback ride into the canyon with an Indian guide. When the day finally arrives, four of us hop on our horses and plod along enjoying the scenery. The guide is a slightly hungover youth who obviously still longs to be in bed. One teacher rides next to him. The scenery is no longer her ultimate enjoyment; she is advising the guide to return to school. By the time the ride is over, she has offered the name of a community college, discussed majors with him, and is convinced she has made a conquest in the name of education. Maybe if I were a braver person, I'd have been on the other side of him offering the name of a church, discussing salvation, and convinced I'd planted a seed. Help me, Lord, to be a braver witness.

# HIDDEN THINGS

*But Jonah ran away from the LORD*
*and headed for Tarshish.*
*He went down to Joppa,*
*where he found a ship bound for that port.*
*After paying the fare,*
*he went aboard and sailed for Tarshish*
*to flee from the LORD.*

JONAH 1:3

Canyon de Chelley is a beautiful place. It still looks very much as it did a hundred years ago. My horse obeys my commands, and I am able to enjoy the landscape and extras. While one from my group recruits our guide, I'm planning future classroom lessons in my head. Another teacher, however, enjoys none of these adventures. She drew the unwilling horse. He absolutely does not want to be on this outing. The four corners desert area is not known for lush trees or much greenery, but her horse manages to find every bush and shrub and hide behind them. Never mind that he's bigger than the foliage. Again and again, the guide patiently retrieves her, nudges her horse forward, and then heads back to lead. Lord, we're often unwilling and don't want to go where you lead us. Thank You for patiently retrieving us again and again. Help us to stay on the narrow road.

# LEFT BEHIND

*And hope does not disappoint us,*
*because God has poured out his love*
*into our hearts by the Holy Spirit,*
*whom he has given us.*

ROMANS 5:5

We're only in Canyon de Chelley for the weekend, and one teacher has a migraine. As the rest of us leave to explore a region we might never visit again, she stays in the motel room and rests. We think about her as we head toward the stable where I've reserved a ride. It's closed. We think of her as we find a different stable, pool our money, and climb onto our horses. It's hard to be left behind. This trip had been planned months ago; the headache was not invited. We all hope she'll feel better by this evening. Lord, each one of us experiences disappointment. We work hard for a goal only to be denied in the final moment. Help us to remember that only one goal holds eternal rewards.

# DUMB LUCK

*I eagerly expect and hope that*
*I will in no way be ashamed,*
*but will have sufficient courage so that now as always*
*Christ will be exalted in my body,*
*whether by life or by death.*

PHILIPPIANS 1:20

It's Saturday evening in a strange town. So far, my tour guide abilities have been met with interest by the group of teachers. I booked the safest-looking motel in the area. I reserved horses at a stable that closed for a day on a whim. Gamely, we moved on to an alternative with ease. I urged everyone to bring a dress-up outfit so that on Saturday evening we could go to a nice restaurant. In Canyon de Chelley, the nice restaurant is Val's Pizza. Although overdressed, we have a great time.  Lord, the unexpected has proved a joyful adventure. Thank You for keeping us safe. Thank You for this opportunity to network, explore, and cement friendships.

# TRY A LITTLE KINDNESS

*I have no greater joy than
to hear that my children
are walking in the truth.*

3 JOHN 4

Father, I thank You that You surround me with children. I spent much of my workday listening to laughter, seeing smiles, and getting hugs. How You've blessed me. Help me, Father, to spread this environment to the rest of my world. Help me to laugh when I want to cry. Help me to smile when I want to curse. Help me to hug those who "need" a hug and not just the people I "like" to hug.

# WHERE THE CAT ROAMS

*Then make my joy complete by*
*being like-minded, having the same love,*
*being one in spirit and purpose.*

PHILIPPIANS 2:2

During the years when I have no students allergic to cats, I some-times bring Aquila to my classroom. He loves it. Fearlessly, he tra-verses the desks, jumping from one to another in search of the perfect napping spot. I watch my students as different expressions cross their faces. Some can imagine no greater joy than sharing their space with my black-and-white, fluffy, fifteen-pound cat. Others like to look at him but don't want to touch. They *want* to like him but would rather not risk any unusual consequences. Aquila always chooses a desk belonging to the latter type of child. It's as if he knows where he isn't welcome and is determined to change that child's mind about the wonders of cats. Lord, so often You went places where You weren't wanted. Thank You, Lord, for choosing not only the safe and welcoming places. Thank You for reaching out to hesitant souls.

# CELEBRATION

*Don't let anyone look down on you
because you are young,
but set an example for the believers in speech,
in life, in love, in faith and in purity.*

1 TIMOTHY 4:12

I took a night class not too long ago, Lord, and for the first assignment, the teacher required us to write a 250-word essay describing who we would invite to a dinner party if we were only allowed ten guests. The day she handed back the assignments, she mentioned that in this upper-level English class, the most desired guest was Jesus. What a privilege, what a joy, to sit in a class surrounded by young people, where I was a returning student and in my forties, and realize that no matter the piercings, tattoos, low-slung jeans, and bare midriffs, Jesus is still present among today's youth. Thank You, Lord, for taking a doubter like me and showing me that the next generation might not be the lost generation.

# BARBIE AND KEN

*"Why do you look at the speck of sawdust
in your brother's eye and pay no attention to
the plank in your own eye?"*

MATTHEW 7:3

I think Ken and Barbie entered my classroom, Lord. He surely
was a high school football star and she a cheerleader. They took
their seats, and over the next few months, I came to realize that not
only are Ken and Barbie pleasing to look at, they are a joy to know.
He treats her with respect and gentleness. She treats him in a con-
genial and nurturing way. They work together. I am in awe. I
assumed that Ken and Barbie were snobs because of their looks,
their dress, and their obvious wealth. How often do I look at a student, Lord, and misjudge him or her based on stereotypes? So
often, Lord, You show me the error of my ways. Lord, help me to
make the choice to keep an open mind about *all* Your children.

# ALLIGATOR SHOES

*"Do not take a purse or bag or sandals."*

LUKE 10:4

Lord, my very first teaching job came with a dress code. For more than five years, I wore dresses, nylons, and nice shoes—not by choice. Eventually, the dress code relaxed, but I'm not sure I ever have. Since that job, I've never been able to shake the belief that looking professional means acting and being professional. And for some reason, Lord, the more professional-looking the clothes, the more professional I feel. It shouldn't be the way I look, but the way I teach, that matters. Still, the way I feel about myself invades my classroom, and I tend to overspend just to look nice. Lord, help me to model self-esteem and professionalism that count. Keep me from thinking that material goods make the difference. After all, You sent out the Seventy-two with only the barest necessities and an urgent message to spread.

## FIRST AND FOREMOST

*If it is leadership,*
*let him govern diligently;*
*if it is showing mercy,*
*let him do it cheerfully.*

· ROMANS 12:8

Look, Lord. My line leader proudly marches down the hall. He knows right where to go because not only have I given him directions (like You give us directions via Your Word, the Holy Bible), but he's led the way before. Wouldn't it be a joy, Lord, if this young man led the way for others to follow You? Look at him, Lord. He is basking in the moment of knowing he's doing it right. He's pleasing others. Let him never lose the ability and desire to take charge—especially of his own life, choosing right over wrong.

# FOLLOW ME

*"In your unfailing love you will
lead the people you have redeemed.
In your strength you will guide them
to your holy dwelling."*

EXODUS 15:13

Moses led the people through the wilderness for forty years. Lord, I cannot even fathom the magnitude of such a wandering. My principal leads a much smaller group of people, and she doesn't carry a staff—just a piece of chalk and a pointer. Lord, I thank You for the people who truly give their all by taking leadership roles in both school and church. It would be impossible to pay them their worth. They are at the front line and make my job (as a teacher and worshiper) easier.

## Be Aware

*But there were also false prophets*
*among the people,*
*just as there will be*
*false teachers among you.*

2 PETER 2:1

Father, it took me a few years of teaching to realize how powerful the leadership of an individual student can be, especially in my college classes. In almost all classes, one individual takes on the center role in the class. My best semesters have been when the class leader was a forward-thinking, motivated, serious student. My challenging semesters have been when the class leader was an uninspiring, unmotivated, less than serious student. Lord, it is such a life lesson. There are some people we are just drawn to. They have charisma. They appear to be leaders, but, in truth, we'd do well to stand on our own feet. Help me, Lord, to lead my students and to work hard to make sure a poor student leader does not gain too much control.

# First, Next, Last

*God had planned something better for us
so that only together with us
would they be made perfect.*

Hebrews 11:40

At the beginning of each school year, Lord, I am handed a lesson-plan book. I look forward to this because I love filling up empty pages with my words. I open the book and look at my five-day week. I have a tiny box for each subject, and I'm supposed to write my plans in it. Sometimes I write everything, and *I write really small.* Sometimes I just write a word or two—to jog my memory. After all, *I know what I'm doing.* Actually, the lesson-plan book is there more for a substitute. Lord, I thank You that Your words are neither small nor limited. A substitute would never be able to figure out exactly what I want from a day—not by my words. But, Lord, if I follow Your Word, I know exactly what to do.

# ENOUGH

*Are you so foolish?*
*After beginning with the Spirit,*
*are you now trying to attain*
*your goal by human effort?*

GALATIANS 3:3

I have my plans for the day laid out in front of me, Lord. My goal is to get everything done. I am a list maker. I love to put check marks by the plans I complete. I've learned, though, through trial and error, that in elementary school it's best to let the children decide what we complete and what we do not complete. I don't mean I let them have a verbal opinion. No, I mean that their attention span and body language help me judge the length of a lesson. Consequently, often what I want to take one day may take a week. Lord, thank You for giving me the ability to watch my students for their "best" time. Keep me from thinking of myself only.

# PAY ATTENTION

*I am not saying this because I am in need,*
*for I have learned to be content*
*whatever the circumstances.*

PHILIPPIANS 4:11

I just taught three classes in a row—same topic, same lesson plan, same level and number of students. The first class was sluggish. It didn't get far, but it's my 7:30 a.m. class, and I'm just as drowsy as the students. My midmorning class got the farthest. They participated. They were alert and even enjoyed some of the activities. My noon class aped my first class, and I want to know why. Lord, I've heard that we each have our own personal favorite "time." I understand my early-morning class. Throughout the years, I've learned to ad-lib a bit more before 8:00 a.m. Lord, why aren't my lessons received by *all* with enthusiasm? What can I do to be more effective? Who should change—me or the students? Am I expecting too much? Am I doing my best, Lord, and can I be content with what I'm doing? How do I know if I'm doing enough?

# Said the Spider to the Fly

*As a prisoner for the Lord, then,*
*I urge you to live a life worthy*
*of the calling you have received.*

EPHESIANS 4:1

Lord, it's a wonder to watch a spider weave its web. The spider painstakingly puts together an intricate weaving designed not only as a home, but as a lure. Scientists recently determined that each web is designed to lure a specific prey. So, if the spider is fond of flies, the web boasts a design specifically for catching flies. Wouldn't it be wonderful, Lord, if teachers had the time to design lesson plans that could lure students? Lord, I thank You for putting together the Bible—specifically to lure me into Your fold.

# Who Took My Crayon?

*My dear brothers, take note of this:*
*Everyone should be quick to listen,*
*slow to speak and slow to become angry.*

JAMES 1:19

I'm angry with the Crayola crayon company. Why? Because they discontinued the color indigo. I'm wondering if anyone else noticed the passing of this color. Elementary teachers should have raised their voices against the loss. Indigo is a very important color. We need indigo. It's the sixth color of the rainbow! I'm not a happy teacher when I pass out my rainbow coloring page and tell my students that although the sixth color is indigo, they'll have to choose a dark blue instead. It doesn't feel right. I don't like substituting. The students really don't care. Maybe I'm the only one who cares. And there are more important things to ge upset over. Help me, Lord, to let go of the little things and dwell on the issues that count.

# THE EARLY BIRD

*But what does it matter?*
*The important thing is that in every way,*
*whether from false motives or true,*
*Christ is preached.*

PHILIPPIANS 1:18

I am always amazed that some students miss the first day of college. It's the most important! It is when the syllabus rules are outlined. It is when the teachers organize the "Get to Know You" activities. It is the only time when every student shares a common ground—first-day nervousness. And, Lord, the excuses I hear. . . Usually the truant student takes weeks to find the flow that the other students discovered on the first day. Lord, I ask that You remind me *often* that what is important is that the student is here *now*. Not everyone hears Your Word when it is spoken; some come later. Thank You, Lord, for second chances.

# Nobody Does It Better

*You, therefore, have no excuse,*
*you who pass judgment on someone else,*
*for at whatever point you judge the other,*
*you are condemning yourself,*
*because you who pass judgment*
*do the same things.*

Romans 2:1

A sub is teaching for me tomorrow, Lord. I've divided my day into hours and minutes and written detailed lesson plans. The sub should have no problem knowing what to do. But, Lord, You know she won't do it the way I do. She'll forget to write the reminder on the board. She'll pronounce a few names wrong. She'll give the students too long for restroom break. She'll probably forget to send them to the library. Maybe I should skip my doctor's appointment, schedule it later, and teach my class. Lord, I'm already convinced that she can't do the job. And I'm wrong. It takes a village to raise a child. It takes a long line of skilled teachers to instruct a student. Lord, let me know when to hang on and when to let go.

# CHOICES

*Let the wise listen and add to their learning,*
*and let the discerning get guidance.*

PROVERBS 1:5

Lord, as I write these prayers, I am reminded again and again how much the children have given me. If I were to write a pros-and-cons list about my years of elementary school teaching, the pros list would require more paper than exists. The cons list would be there, but much shorter. Lord, it bothers me that the cons list is a vivid memory while the pros list—*the longer list*—is of memories that come and go. Lord, teach me to dwell on the positive, learn from the negative, and change what I can.

# Taking the Time
# to Do It Right

*Everyone should be quick to listen,*
*slow to speak and slow to become angry.*

James 1:19

He cried for four days, Lord. I didn't know what to do. I praised, cajoled, and soothed until I ran out of ideas. I forgot to look at Your Word. Finally, in the women's restroom, while drying his eyes, I ran out of words. And I listened to this small boy who spoke limited English and didn't know our culture. He didn't really want to talk, but I think my silence made him nervous. No one had told him, Lord. No one knew how to tell him. He was frightened because every morning when his mother dropped him off, he had no assurance she would return to pick him up. "School ends at three," I told him. "Mothers always return to pick students up." Then he was happy. Thank You, Lord, for giving me the opportunity to listen. Help me, Lord, to learn to listen more and talk less. And always, always, keep anger out of my classroom.

# IMPLY/INFER

*"He who has ears, let him hear."*

MATTHEW 11:15

Lord, when I say to one of my students, "Tell your mother I need to speak with her," fear clouds the child's face. Actually, all I need to do is firm up plans for the mother's visit to our class. Quickly, I reassure the child and wonder how so young a student got the preconceived notion that a teacher wanting to speak with a parent is *always* a bad thing. As I am wondering, the first-grade teacher pokes her head in my door. "The principal needs to talk with you," she tells me. "Oh," I respond. "What did I do wrong?" Lord, help me to not always assume the worst. I need to be an example for my students who also assume the worst.

# BECAUSE I SAID SO

*Do not merely listen to the word,*
*and so deceive yourselves.*
*Do what it says.*

JAMES 1:22

Why?" It's a question I hear often from students, Lord. I understand, from teachers who've been around longer than I, that at one time students simply said, "Yes, ma'am." So often, in education, students want to know why they have to perform a certain duty. Why do they need to know the times tables? Why is the capital of Nebraska important to know? Why is the fourth president vital to their existence? Sometimes I have a definite answer; other times it's "just because." Lord, I often ask You why. Why am I fat? Why did my mother die? Why do I have to go to church three times a week? Lord, help me to follow You because *I want to.* Let me be a "Yes, Lord," follower and not a "Why, Lord?" doubter.

# LOUDMOUTH

*"Blessed are the meek,*
*for they will inherit the earth."*

MATTHEW 5:5

Lord, so often in a group, I try to manipulate the conversation. I recognize this flaw in my personality, but sometimes I am not bright enough to control it. Other people are trying to talk, and I'm interrupting them because I *think* I know more than they do. Lord, I am afraid that if I were in a group with You, I might not be sensible enough to stop talking long enough to listen. Lord, so often this trait has cost me the respect of others—students, parents, peers, administrators—and I need to conquer the high opinion I have of myself. Help me, Lord, to live according to Your will.

# AGENDAS

*Do your best to present yourself
to God as one approved,
a workman who does not need to be ashamed
and who correctly handles the word of truth.*

2 TIMOTHY 2:15

The meeting begins. Gathered around me are the decision-makers. *What am I doing in this room?* The president of the school board begins. I am number seven on the agenda. I've prepared my argument and am to be the expert on one side of the issue. I do not feel like an expert. My turn comes. I clear my throat and begin. Lord, there are times when I have to stand among those I deem more important, worthier, more knowledgeable than I. Thank You, Lord, for giving me the strength to present my case. Thank You for opportunities to listen and learn about others' opinions. Thank You for leaders who know more than I.

# COME TO ORDER

*"For where two or three come together in my name,*
*there am I with them."*

MATTHEW 18:20

Very seldom does a group of teachers meet and *not* discuss how to make things better. We want our students prepared. We want our textbooks well written and manageable. We want success for every student. Everyone has ideas, and for some odd reason, Lord, often the ideas of one do not complement the others. Lord, help us when we meet to discuss things in a rational and productive way. Help us put aside the wants and focus on the needs. Help us to always work together toward the goal of educating today's youth.

# WE GATHER TOGETHER

*Let us not give up meeting together,*
*as some are in the habit of doing,*
*but let us encourage one another—*
*and all the more as you see the Day approaching.*

HEBREWS 10:25

We gather for our official first meeting of the school year. A roomful of teachers starts by praying about sick students, divorcing parents, and, of course, money problems. Next, we decide on yearly projects—like collecting food for the needy. Then we delegate more school-related tasks—like motivational projects to get our students reading. Last, our principal looks for volunteers. *Who will do the September bulletin board? Who will make up a duty roster for the year?* Oh, it's good to be back, Lord. Thank you for teamwork. Let me be a help, not a hindrance. I tend to be bossy, Lord, and think I can do better than the next person. You often prove this theory wrong. Help me to learn from others and to step back and accept orders when my natural tendency is to give them.

# COMMITTEES

*For we are God's workmanship,*
*created in Christ Jesus to do good works,*
*which God prepared in advance for us to do.*

EPHESIANS 2:10

The chair of our department calls the meeting to order and begins. He has an agenda with almost twenty items. Some we'll spend quite a bit of time on because they concern everyone. Other items we'll parcel out. When parceling out, the key word is "committees." I've been on committees that were wonderful. We all worked together toward a common goal. Then, I've been on committees where a few did the work while many got the glory. Lord, help me in the future, when I serve on committees, to be a dependable worker. Allow me to be a help and not a hindrance.

# THEY COMFORT ME

*Is any one of you in trouble?*
*He should pray.*
*Is anyone happy?*
*Let him sing songs of praise.*

JAMES 5:13

Lord, I have the unique opportunity to attend church in the building where I teach school. What a joy to teach at a Christian school! I'm surrounded by mentors who walk the walk, talk the talk, and lead by example. They are humble while I am haughty. I always need the spiritual and professional guidance they offer. Lord, my prayer is that I never cause another—be it student, parent, or peer—to stumble. I am in a position that can sometimes (*often*) be stressful. There are times when I dread going to church because I know that one of Your flock is unhappy about the events of a single day—*unhappy with me*. Sometimes the school day spills over into the worship setting. Lord, help me to be the teacher You hope for Your children. I thank You for mentors who surround me and comfort me and pray for me.

# EXAMPLES

*Don't let anyone look down on you*
*because you are young,*
*but set an example for the believers in speech,*
*in life, in love, in faith and in purity.*

1 TIMOTHY 4:12

I was raised as an only child, Lord. I really don't know how to argue, and I struggle to freely give in to the concept of sharing. If I share, I want recognition. As I walk down the halls of my school and look at the teachers working in their offices, I'm reminded that I'm surrounded by greatness. Yes, Lord, greatness. I've been blessed with the company of many master teachers. These ladies and gentlemen show up for work every day; they buy classroom supplies with their own money; they give up afternoons for tutoring; they give up evenings for drama practice; and they stand outside in the rain to give time to a parent who wants to talk. I am the least of them. They, like Jesus, are my mentors.

# INSTRUCTIONS

*Be diligent in these matters;*
*give yourself wholly to them,*
*so that everyone may see your progress.*
*Watch your life and doctrine closely.*
*Persevere in them, because if you do,*
*you will save both yourself and your hearers.*

1 TIMOTHY 4:15–16

In the Bible, Lord, we are treated to the examples of Paul and Timothy. Paul must have been quite a dynamic man. He dominates (both as writer and participant) much of the history we are privy to in the New Testament. Paul had a young assistant named Timothy whom he called "my true son in the faith." What a compliment. Lord, I'd like to thank You for my mentors. These older, wiser women took me under their wings when I was a young teacher who knew nothing about the realities of being in a classroom. I am a better teacher because of their examples. I have had many Pauls throughout my teaching career. I pray I have many more. And I pray that I do the same for the younger teachers looking to me for guidance.

# SHE'S THE ONE

*I planted the seed,*
*Apollos watered it,*
*but God made it grow.*

1 CORINTHIANS 3:6

Lord, the first time I met her she was a first grader—long golden hair, princess dress, and always a smile. Throughout the years, she has been my student helper, my young assistant during summer school, and even the young lady I mentioned when someone asked me to recommend a babysitter. The last time I saw her she was a newlywed—long golden hair, neatly pressed pantsuit, and always a smile. Today she is a teacher. Lord, I'd like to think I was an influence, but probably not. From first grade until today, she has been one of Your children. She's the happily-ever-after student who lives the way You meant us to live.

# Oops

*Every good and perfect gift is from above,*
*coming down from the Father*
*of the heavenly lights,*
*who does not change like shifting shadows.*

JAMES 1:17

There's a stack of one hundred handouts that I'm going to pass out to my English composition students tomorrow, Lord. I wrote it yesterday, edited it last night, and copied it off this morning. I'm prepared. Except—what's that? In the middle of the page is a major typographical error. It changes everything! Should I redo the whole paper? Use this batch as scrap? Or should I tell the students, "I'm not perfect and here's proof." Lord, sometimes no matter how often I look at a project, I miss the obvious errors. Lord, I thank You that when You see my human errors, my sins, You are not expecting perfection. Thank You for forgiving me.

# WHERE THE HEART TAKES YOU

*If it is serving, let him serve;*
*if it is teaching, let him teach.*

ROMANS 12:7

Lord, there are days I leave the classroom and know You meant for me to be a teacher. There are also days when I leave the classroom and I wonder how You ever made such a mistake. A teacher? Me? When something goes wrong in my day, I gnaw on the mistake until it's all I can think of. I often blame others. I let the unfortunate occurrence shadow my every move. I start second-guessing my decisions until all the joy seeps out of teaching. Lord, let me learn from my mistakes. And let me always look toward You as my example.

# Pop Quiz

*Be prepared in season and out of season;*
*correct, rebuke and encourage—*
*with great patience and careful instruction.*

2 Timothy 4:2

I gave a quiz today, Lord. In a class of twenty college students, only three were prepared. *They'd* read the story. I watched the students who turned in blank papers. Some were surely thinking, *Okay, I need to make sure I read from now on.* Others were perhaps thinking, *Reading is stupid.* And still a few were probably thinking, *Unfair! Unfair! Unfair!* Lord, opportunity is a blessed thing. I thank You for a society where education is available to all who knock. Please, Lord, be with the students who are young, immature, and careless. Let them learn from their mistakes, Lord, and strive for high learning.

# A HUMAN MOMENT

*I do not understand what I do.*
*For what I want to do I do not do,*
*but what I hate I do.*
*And if I do what I do not want to do,*
*I agree that the law is good.*

ROMANS 7:15–16

In ten minutes, we leave on a field trip, Lord. Ten minutes ago a driver called. Her child is sick. The principal and parents and students are looking at me. By rearranging, I can place all but two students. Do I cancel the field trip? Do I put the two children in front seats? It's against the law because my students weigh less than sixty pounds, and my spare seats both have air bags. Lord, I'm afraid that if it were up to me—and if no one were looking—I might make a mistake and put a child in the front passenger seat. Lord, because I am human, I err so often. I'm thankful I have You to listen to and Your Word to guide me. I am thankful for laws that make me think twice.

# MORNING STARS

*They are new every morning;*
*great is your faithfulness.*

LAMENTATIONS 3:23

It's morning, Lord. The students bend over their lessons. I see a few yawns. It's time to get this day started right! I clap my hands. "Let's go outside," I say. Here in the crisp air, I see pink flushing on the cheeks of my surprised class. Some days when I bring them out, I am structured. We play Duck, Duck, Goose. Other times, I simply chase them. Me, in my open-toed sandals and long, flapping skirt. They, in their tennis shoes, jeans, and cotton shirts. Today I just let them play. They scramble like ants over the playground equipment. For some reason, my loners are more willing to socialize in the morning. In the afternoon, when the heat of the day is upon us, they might swing in solitude or circle the playground alone, searching for something or someone they might never find. You gave us mornings. Lord, let us use each brand-new day wisely.

# TIME IN THE CAR

> *" 'He is like the light of morning*
> *at sunrise on a cloudless morning,*
> *like the brightness after rain*
> *that brings the grass from the earth.' "*

2 SAMUEL 23:4

Sometimes, Lord, on my way to school in the morning, I am so at peace in my car. I am heading for a classroom where a troop of children depend on me to make their day. Lord, contentment often flows through me as I look forward to the greetings, hugs, and excitement that might occur. I get my best ideas in the car as I imagine the day's lessons. I decide whom I'm going to call on. I actually try to remember the previous day to see if any child didn't receive enough of my attention. Thank You for mornings that start each day anew. Thank You for a chance to make a difference. You are my example.

# WAKING UP

*They are new every morning;*
*great is your faithfulness.*

LAMENTATIONS 3:23

I am not a morning person, Lord. Consequently, I live in fear of oversleeping and missing my 7:30 class. I own three alarm clocks, and I always set more than one. First, I am sure that if only *one* went off, I might not hear it. Next, I might accidentally turn *one* off when I think I'm hitting the snooze, so I always set a spare. Eventually, I want to color code my alarm clocks. As a college professor, my classes are staggered throughout the week. I want my white alarm clock to wake me up on Mondays and Wednesdays. I want my black alarm clock to wake me up on Tuesdays and Thursdays. I want my red alarm clock for my Friday class. Lord, I'm worried about my priorities. If I am this diligent when it comes to getting to work on time, help me to do the same for Sunday morning services.

# CLEAN SLATE

*In the morning, O LORD,*
*you hear my voice;*
*in the morning I lay my requests before you*
*and wait in expectation.*

PSALM 5:3

Lord, mornings are like the whiteboard that is clean of any markings —especially on the very first day of school. No harsh words have been uttered. No friendships have been damaged. No mistakes have been noted by all. There has been no time for judgments based on past performance. Mornings glitter with the potential for opportunity. Lord, remind me to embrace each morning and to greet my students as if this will be the best day of their lives— every day.

# MATTHEW, MARK, LUKE, AND JOHN

*"Rejoice that your names
are written in heaven."*

LUKE 10:20

There are five Christophers in this class, Lord. Three of them have last names that begin with M. Throughout my day, I encounter four Ashleys (Ashleigh, Ashly, Ashlee). All expect me to remember the correct spelling of their names. There is a student in my 7:30 a.m. class with a name that consists only of consonants. He patiently states, restates, and restates *again* his name, but I never repeat it back to him correctly. Lord, our names brand us. They are important. I've never taught a Judas. That name is branded; it means "traitor." I've taught many Marks, Georges, Marys, and Elizabeths. Those are solid names, dependable. In teacher workshops, they tell us that learning a student's name is one way of motivating a student to stay in school. Lord, I am so thankful that You know my name.

# HONEST LABOR

*You will eat the fruit of your labor;*
*blessings and prosperity will be yours.*

PSALM 128:2

Lord, that bumper sticker reads: "My Child Is an Honor Roll Student at. . ." I hope someday to have one on the bumper of my car. But I also hope I remember the value of the letter grade C. It has a reputation it doesn't deserve. For some reason, in today's society a C just isn't acceptable. A C means average, and we don't want our children to be average. Here's a teacher's truth. I'm more impressed by a student who works hard for a C than I am by a student who receives an A and never had to try. Lord, let us value the honest labor of the student, not just the letter grade. Help me, as a teacher, to remember that.

# NOW

*"Sow for yourselves righteousness,*
*reap the fruit of unfailing love,*
*and break up your unplowed ground;*
*for it is time to seek the LORD, until he comes*
*and showers righteousness on you."*

HOSEA 10:12

My college students are working in groups, Lord. I sit on top of an old teacher's desk in the back of the room. There's a box of papers and odds and ends that have occupied this desk since I started teaching in this room, oh, maybe six years ago. The students do not need me, so I sort through the stack. A brochure advertising a grammar workshop that took place two years ago is on top. Then someone's graded math paper from 1999. I find what looks like mimeographed copies of an Edgar Allan Poe story. A spiral notebook missing half its pages is at the bottom. A student raises his hand, and I leave the box to start teaching again. Lord, sometimes, like the owner of this used spiral, I forget where I've placed Your Word. Often, I'm still working on an issue that should have been resolved or discarded back in 1999. Help me to move forward and do Your will now.

# CHRISTIAN EXAMPLES

*Be shepherds. . .*
*not lording it over those entrusted to you,*
*but being examples to the flock.*

1 PETER 5:2–3

Some of my best friends are teachers, Lord. Most, if not all, are better teachers than I am. They are smarter, kinder, quicker to think of the right response, better nurturers, and more thoughtful than I can ever hope to be. Sometimes I listen to the way they talk to students, parents, and other teachers, and I think, *Why can't I be more like them?* Lord, I thank You for the gift of examples that motivate me to try to be a better Christian, teacher, and friend. I've learned so much from them. Lord, help me to learn more.

# WHAT SAY YOU?

*Who are you to judge someone else's servant?*
*To his own master he stands or falls.*
*And he will stand,*
*for the Lord is able to make him stand.*

ROMANS 14:4

In my classroom this year is a special-needs student. I have the paperwork that indicates I should make special accommodations for him. Lord, one example of how I meet his needs is that instead of giving him thirty spelling words, I'm to give him ten. When I grade papers, I'm to give him an A if he gets all ten correct, just like I'm to give an A to the other students who get all thirty correct. It's a form of negotiation. Lord, I'm never sure what happens when the students go out into the world. There are two sides to the issues. If we expect less from a student, we should not be surprised at a less than stellar performance. If we expect more than they can give, we should not be surprised when they quit. Lord, I want to thank You for the authority figures who make decisions when I cannot. Thank You that we live in a time when a student's disabilities are dealt with instead of ignored.

# LITTLE HELPERS

*In everything set them an example by doing*
*what is good. In your teaching show integrity,*
*seriousness and soundness of speech*
*that cannot be condemned.*

TITUS 2:7–8

One of my students broke her leg and is in a wheelchair. This is big news in first grade. Everyone wants to be the helper to navigate the wheelchair. The little girl is trusting. Me? I'm more concerned about a sore foot smashing into a corner or a door closing on the cast. Our politically correct textbooks always contain a visual of someone in a wheelchair. But, Lord, peers are not always the best ones for guidance, so we negotiate. Down a straight hall, I allow them to slowly push her, but I take over for the long haul, just as the adult should. To make them happy, we spend a bit more time in the hall so they all get a turn. In exchange, they finish their work quickly and quietly. Never has the hallway been so much fun. Lord, in a world where peers are sometimes a more important example than adults, thank You for the opportunity to combine responsibility with teaching.

# NO MAN IS AN ISLAND

*"May the LORD keep watch between you and me
when we are away from each other."*

GENESIS 31:49

Father, to the parent, it probably seems a simple request. To the teacher, it's never simple. Missing weeks of school is a dilemma with no "perfect" solution. So often, I've gathered together papers and lesson plans to hand over to a parent who assures me it will be done. And just as often a stack of papers returns one-third complete. I'm as guilty. I also fail my end of the negotiation. I give parents two weeks of work; they diligently sit down and instruct their child; and when they return, they discover the class is two chapters ahead in science and one chapter behind in math. Lord, missing school is a bit like missing church. I never feel quite with it when I return. Watch over me and my students, Lord, when we are apart from each other.

# FINAL GRADES

*Perseverance must finish its work*
*so that you may be mature and complete,*
*not lacking anything.*

JAMES 1:4

Lord, sometimes a student will remind me of the movie *Clueless*. In one scene, the heroine earns a grade she believes is unacceptable, so she goes to the instructor and negotiates a new grade. Persuasion skills instead of academic skills prevail. Sometimes I think my students have seen this movie, forgotten its title, and believe grades are negotiable. Take the student who sat across from me one day after finals and tried to convince me that perfect attendance was just as important as turning in assignments. The student had excellent verbal skills. What she didn't have was a class average that was anywhere near passing. Lord, I felt awful when the student left—as if I were responsible for her poor choices. As always, I ask for guidance to know when to bend and when to stand firm.

# SAY "A"

*"I tell you the truth,
until heaven and earth disappear,
not the smallest letter,
not the least stroke of a pen,
will by any means disappear from the Law
until everything is accomplished."*

MATTHEW 5:18

Today, Lord, all around the classroom are pictures of items beginning with the letter *A*. Students will eat apple slices. They'll color alligators. They'll glue noodles onto a giant letter *A*. They will read sentences and circle every *A* they see—noting which need to be uppercase compared to which need to be lowercase. When they leave, they'll carry with them a stapled collection of *A* papers. They'll also carry home *A* flash cards, and I envision eager parents doing the *ah, ay, ar, aw* sounds. The students enjoy days that center around one simple focus. Lord, I enjoy these days, too. I can hardly wait for tomorrow, *B* day. I'll put a picture of the Bible up. We'll read from the Bible. And *G* day will be here soon! And *J*! Thank You, Lord, for putting me in a school where You can be a whole lesson.

# BURIED ALIVE

*"Then you will know the truth,*
*and the truth will set you free."*

JOHN 8:32

I didn't assign any homework, Lord, but in class we brainstormed ideas for future writings. Our next class period, a student stayed after to confess he'd *thought* I assigned something, wasn't sure what, and *since* he wrote something, would I mind looking at it? I've been a teacher a long time, Lord. The fact that he didn't understand my instructions set off warning bells. Still, I read his paragraph, and it's what I feared. The paragraph demonstrates that he doesn't belong in my class, and it would be hard to offer any positive advice. It's hard to tell the truth to students. I never want my words to stop a student from striving forward. On the other hand, it's important to tell students that there's a certain order to education. Lord, are there really teachers out there who always know the right words to say? Help me, Lord, to be more like them.

# A GUIDING LIGHT

*Let the wise listen and add to their learning,*
*and let the discerning get guidance.*

PROVERBS 1:5

It takes me awhile to put names to faces, Lord. Once I've mastered recognition, I start sorting through the paper trails that follow students. I check to see their placement scores. I look at the grades they've earned in previous classes. Every once in a while, I find a student who doesn't belong in my class. Either he passed the class last semester and simply forgot he'd "been there; done that" (I'm not sure how this can happen but it does), or he belongs in a prerequisite that he was hoping nobody would notice he neglected to take. Either way, I wind up adding to the paper trail by gathering schedule-adjustment forms or waiver sheets. I try to guide the student to where he belongs. Lord, You've always known my name and face. I, too, often wind up in the wrong place. I thank You for Your guidance.

# SEEKING THE LOST

*Plans fail for lack of counsel,*
*but with many advisers they succeed.*

PROVERBS 15:22

I mean to be an organized person. I color code and alphabetize and buy all kinds of files and boxes, but truthfully, I wind up with stacks of paper everywhere—everywhere except where they are supposed to be—and I waste valuable time searching for what should be neatly filed away. Lately, I've been meaning to buy new file folders. I'm just sure sturdy, unused folders will inspire me to keep better track of my students' paperwork. Scattered on my desk are permission slips, parent notes, exceptional papers, discipline reports, and much more. Help me to stop putting off what must be done, Father.

# SPIT WADS

*"He who has ears, let him hear."*

MATTHEW 11:15

Four little boys sit in front of me, Lord. They were caught in the restroom tossing spit wads at the ceiling. My first thought is: *Why couldn't it have been the second-grade boys?* My next thought is: *How do I handle it now?* And my last thought is: *What do I tell the parents?* With some parents, I simply pick up the phone, tell them what happened, and they deal with it. Other parents ask who else was involved, and they are sure that their child was coerced into poor behavior choices. And, still, some parents will believe that either their child was not involved—at all—or they'll chuckle and say, "Oh, I did that when I was that age." Lord, saying the correct words to get the same message across to different types of parents is a skill in itself. I ask for courage to speak the truth and for a receiving heart to hear the truth.

# NO SECRETS

*"So you must obey them*
*and do everything they tell you.*
*But do not do what they do,*
*for they do not practice what they preach."*

MATTHEW 23:3

I'm sitting here grading papers, and soon I'll come across the homework of first-grade student, third row, seat four. I know she did her homework because I can smell it. The aroma of her mother's evening cigarettes wafts to my nostrils. Lord, I wonder if parents really know what an open book their private lives are. Especially in the elementary school setting. Teachers are privy to more than they want to know. I know when strangers spend the night; I know which parents say bad words; I know who has had their electricity turned off. Lord, I pray for these students whose parents expect them to "Do what I say, not what I do."

# One + One = Two

*"But many who are first will be last,
and many who are last will be first."*

Matthew 19:30

I have a student whose mother speaks very limited English, yet she shows up in my classroom once a week to help. At first, I wasn't sure what to do with her. Then I realized she was the answer to a prayer. Now, every Thursday morning she sits in the hallway with small groups of children and goes over subtraction and addition facts. I hear my children chanting their answers. I hear her gentle voice encourage them: "Four, yes, four." Lord, I thank You for parents who want to help. This mother expects no plaque with her name on it. She needs no flowers. She doesn't expect me to write a letter to the school board commending her. All she wants is for her child to get the best education possible and for her child to know that Mom was there. Lord, I cherish this mother and her time.

# DRINK YOUR MILK

*"When you enter a town and are welcomed,
eat what is set before you."*

LUKE 10:8

There's an uneaten sandwich in the lunchroom trash can. Pristine in appearance, I just know some mother lovingly packed it this morning. It probably shared its ride to school with a bag of chips, an apple, a cookie, and a juice box. Sounds like a good lunch for an active student. I'm sure the cookie is being digested right about now. Parents load lunch boxes with the best of intentions. Teachers walk around and encourage students to eat with the best of intentions. Lord, thank You for good intentions. Help us to always strive toward them. Help the students value what has been given them.

# BRAND-NEW

*You were taught. . .*
*to be made new in the attitude of your minds;*
*and to put on the new self,*
*created to be like God*
*in true righteousness and holiness.*

EPHESIANS 4:22–24

Lord, the first year I taught kindergarten, I had a class of fifteen boys and five girls. It was a great year. The children didn't know that I was a novice teacher. They didn't know that because I wanted to do a good job, I taught them everything—including some things the first-grade teacher really wanted to teach them. Lord, how can I maintain that enthusiasm? How do I, decades later, keep the same things from feeling old, redundant? Lord, help me find the patience to teach each class as if it were that first class.

# HURRY UP!

*The Lord is not slow in keeping his promise,*
*as some understand slowness.*
*He is patient with you,*
*not wanting anyone to perish,*
*but everyone to come to repentance.*

2 PETER 3:9

We're walking down the hallway, Lord. I have two straight lines—a boy line and a girl line. Looking past the troop of children, I see my straggler. He's just now rounding the corner. As a class, we gathered our belongings, lined up, and began walking. By himself, he slowly put away his pencil, slowly pushed in his chair, and slowly meandered for the door. Oh, I always know where he is. I know when he's on math problem 3 and the rest of the class is on math problem 33. I know when he's taken one bite of his hamburger and the rest of the students have finished all their fries. Lord, I ask You to watch over this little one who has his own concept of time. He's a bright child, Lord, and it takes patience to wait for him. He's going to surprise me someday, and the meticulous way he deals with life will be rewarded.

# Not Again

*Preach the Word;*
*be prepared in season and out of season;*
*correct, rebuke and encourage—*
*with great patience and careful instruction.*

2 Timothy 4:2

Lord, I just called on a student to answer a simple question. She mumbled a strange and incorrect answer and ducked her head. I quickly move to another student and another question, trying not to embarrass her. I continue my lesson, making sure that once, twice, three times more I broach the concept she didn't comprehend. Then I return to her and give her another chance. She misses it again, Lord. How could she miss it? I went over it three times; I wrote it on the board; I had the students read it aloud; I had them get in groups and analyze it. Lord, how often do You wonder the same thing? You've told us, shown us, reminded us about Your ways, and yet we do strange and incorrect things. Thank You for having patience with us and for sending Your Son to help us.

# Aa, Bb, Cc

*The end of a matter is better than its beginning,*
*and patience is better than pride.*

ECCLESIASTES 7:8

Four children stand in front of my chalkboard, Lord. We're working on the letter *A*. Child number one doesn't waste any time. He quickly finishes. Child number two is still working. Child number three checks to see what child number one did. Child number two erases and starts again. Child number four finishes his *A* and returns to his seat without realizing he's missed the lines. Child number two glances up at the ABC chart, studies it for a moment, and returns to his letter. Child number three changes the color of his chalk midletter. Child number two redoes the tip of his *A*. Eventually, four capital *A*'s are displayed. Lord, the student who was patient has the best *A*. Teach me patience, Lord. I need to teach lessons, start over, and teach again. I need to study my students' skills and learning styles. I need to pay attention to strengths and weaknesses. Patience will make me a better teacher.

# Wolf in Sheep's Clothing

*No temptation has seized you except*
*what is common to man.*
*And God is faithful;*
*he will not let you be tempted beyond what you can bear.*
*But when you are tempted,*
*he will also provide a way out*
*so that you can stand up under it.*

1 Corinthians 10:13

Lord, one year a misguided student was in my night class. He even wore a name tag proclaiming himself as Satan. I cannot imagine the baggage he carried that made him want such attention. He did not fit in with his peers. He was not a typical student. Satan earned a C in my class. He didn't want to do much of anything except annoy others—we were always grateful when he was absent—and did just enough to get by. I think the real Satan probably isn't so lackadaisical. The real Satan is always busy thinking of ways to trip up people. I was grateful when the semester was over and Satan, the student, was out of my life. I wish the real Satan would only pester me a semester and then disappear so easily and thoroughly. Thank You for Your promise that Satan cannot pester me more than I can handle.

# HERE

*John answered,*
*"The man with two tunics should share*
*with him who has none,*
*and the one who has food should do the same."*

LUKE 3:11

Lord, I have yet to meet a teacher who isn't in love with pens. I love pens—colored pens, sparkly pens, pens in animal shapes. . . If I'm at the bank and the pen I'm using to fill out my deposit writes smoothly—I want it. Because of this addiction, I have drawers full of pens. Some of them no longer work, if they ever did. When someone wants to borrow a pen, I sometimes take a moment to find a pen that isn't a favorite. After all, who thinks to return a pen? My students love crayons, and they teach me an example in sharing. If someone shouts, "I need a black," immediately five peers are out of their seats and offering the color. Thank You for these children, Lord, who show me that if I have twenty pens in my drawer and someone else has none, I should be the first to offer—without choosing my least favorite pen.

# The Closing of a Door

*"To one he gave five talents of money,*
*to another two talents,*
*and to another one talent,*
*each according to his ability."*

MATTHEW 25:15

It's early in the morning, Lord, and I am the first one here. I walk down the hallway toward my office. The doors to all the offices are closed. I am struck by how the personality of each teacher is demonstrated by what he or she has done to the office doors. Some are untouched, not even a fingerprint dare a blemish. A few have important college-related announcements. Others display a single piece of artwork, like a poster of the Grand Canyon. A few have personal photos or cartoons collaged over every inch. I am new faculty, and only half my door is cartooned. In a few years, there will be no door showing. Lord, I've heard it said that it takes a village to raise a child. I thank You for the village of unique personalities who share my profession. I learn something from each of them, but I learn the most from You.

# THE TINIEST BIT

*" 'Well done, good and faithful servant!*
*You have been faithful with a few things;*
*I will put you in charge of many things.' "*

MATTHEW 25:23

Lord, sometimes I feel inadequate in the presence of my peers. They are so together, so talented, so organized. And me, I'm such a struggler. I hang back when I should push forward. Like the other day. A little girl tripped and fell. Blood flowed from a cut on her forehead. All the together, talented, organized teachers rushed to assist. And me, I just stood there wondering what to do. Finally, I blew my whistle and herded the rest of the day-care children to my classroom, where I let them choose centers and games or chalkboard time. My contribution was not as glamorous as the teacher who immediately knew how to stop the bleeding. My help was not as immediate as the teacher who thought to phone the parent. Lord, thank You for letting me help others in small ways. Help me remember that we all have our strengths.

# SEND JESUS RIGHT OVER

*"But if I do judge,*
*my decisions are right,*
*because I am not alone.*
*I stand with the Father,*
*who sent me."*

JOHN 8:16

Red Rover, Red Rover, send. . ." Lord, I'm sure most of us played Red Rover on the playground. I know I did. Now, as an adult watching my students play, I realize the game hasn't changed. Children hold hands and hope that the runner doesn't aim for them because it will hurt, and if the runner gets through, it's their fault. If my students are not holding hands, they're running. They look for a weakness in the chain of hand-holders. I've seen students let go of their partners' hands just so the runner can run through free. Lord, Satan is something like the runner in the game of Red Rover. He looks for the weakest—the one who will let go of Your hand. Lord, give us the strength to stand firm.

# FREE-FALLING

*Be on your guard;*
*stand firm in the faith;*
*be men of courage;*
*be strong.*

1 CORINTHIANS 16:13

Lord, the new teacher next to me flinches and looks to see what I'm going to do. A child has fallen to the ground from the top of the monkey bars. I stand still and wait. A moment passes, and he's up and climbing back to the top. This patience to stand while a little one stumbles used to be alien to me. My first impulse was to run over and offer assistance—without giving the child a chance to stand on his own. Now I realize, Lord, that my students learn best when I allow them to learn from and fix their mistakes. I watch my future Olympic hopeful navigate the monkey bars. This time he holds on with *both* hands.

# PERIMETERS

*"For the Son of Man came to seek
and to save what was lost."*

LUKE 19:10

Our school has a really large playground, Lord. In fact, if an adventurous child wanders too far, he'll soon be out of sight. We've made rules about the perimeter of the playground. If a child ventures too close to the outer edge, we blow our whistle. If the child doesn't hear the whistle, then off we go, running across the playground to make sure we keep our charges close to us. The outer edge has potential dangers like garbage, broken glass, and wire. Lord, when our students leave the safe haven of school, often their lives are one big outer edge full of dangers far worse than a discarded beer can. Guide the children as they travel in a world bursting with pitfalls. Thank You, Lord, for being a Savior who wants to keep Your charges close to You.

# NOAH'S ARK

*The LORD then said to Noah,*
*"Go into the ark, you and your whole family,*
*because I have found you righteous*
*in this generation."*

GENESIS 7:1

Lord, one year my sixth graders and I surveyed the playground fence. It encases the playground, flanks the softball field, shields the deserted lot that we claim will someday be utilized more fully, and even separates us from the parking lot. With our Bibles in hand, we study Genesis, the seventh chapter. With the yards of ribbon I've purchased, we begin measuring 450 feet. I had told them the ark was longer than a football field, and as we continue determining length, I can see by their faces, they no longer doubt me. Finally, we finish. For the next couple of days, I watch my sixth graders, during recess, grandly explaining our length of ribbon to their peers. Then it rains, and the ribbons blow away. Lord, thank You for lessons that allow us to combine math, P.E., and the Bible. Thank You for opportunities to make Your lessons more real.

# In Her Footsteps

*Instead, it should be that of your inner self,*
*the unfading beauty of a gentle and quiet spirit,*
*which is of great worth in God's sight.*

1 Peter 3:4

There is a beautiful teacher at my school, Lord. She is always put together—physically, mentally, and spiritually. One day a little first grader summed up my impression of this gracious teacher. The first grader said, "Teacher, I like you, but I want to be like Mrs. X when I grow up." Lord, I want to be like Mrs. X when I grow up, too. Oh, wait a minute. I am grown-up! Lord, thank You so much for role models like Mrs. X. She is a teacher worthy of praise because she is one of Your children, and she is doing Your work.

# SUPERSTARS

*" 'Well done, good and faithful servant!' "*

MATTHEW 25:21

I am a list maker, and this year, Lord, taped in the front of my address book are the names and phone numbers of my current students. My goal throughout the year is to call each parent to tell of something spectacular achievement his or her child has achieved. Children need compliments, Lord, and to my shame, if I don't keep a list, I might call one parent twenty times with good news and another parent only once. Lord, help me never to overlook one of Your children because of poor memory and missed opportunity. Thank You for teaching me to look for the positives!

# Forgotten Heroes

*Finally, brothers, whatever is true,*
*whatever is noble, whatever is right,*
*whatever is pure, whatever is lovely,*
*whatever is admirable—*
*if anything is excellent or praiseworthy—*
*think about such things.*

Philippians 4:8

As a teacher, Lord, I know how much I value the praise that comes my way, and I'm feeling a bit guilty today. When I was a student, I doubt very much if I said thank you to the teachers who inspired me the most. Right now I'm thinking about my high school history teacher. He so impacted me that I still remember his name. I wonder if he's still teaching. I wonder if he's happy. I wonder if more mature students than I let him know what a wonderful job he was doing. *Job?* That is such an inadequate word for a true, dedicated teacher. Lord, thank You for teachers who shape minds, stretch imaginations, challenge thinking, and mold character.

# A WINNER

*An honest answer is like a kiss on the lips.*

PROVERBS 24:26

Lord, one of the items I miss the most, now that I'm a college professor instead of an elementary teacher, is the power of the sticker. In the days when I guided students third grade and under, I had a whole drawerful of praise stickers. I had one for every occasion: "Well Done!" "Keep Trying," "Excellent," "Perfect," "Be Neater." Even if the sticker wasn't declaring the student a winner, the message was usually accepted in a positive way. In college, my pen and my words are the only encouragement the students will see. When I'm at a loss for words, I don't have a sticker to help me out. Lord, as I'm grading and dealing with students, help me to remember to praise as well as critique. Let me see the good in every attempt.

# MORE AND MORE

*And this is my prayer:*
*that your love may abound more and more*
*in knowledge and depth of insight.*

PHILIPPIANS 1:9

As I grow older, Lord, I draw prayer around me like a favorite comforter. It warms me and gives me security. It constantly reminds me that You are by my side. I listen to my students pray, and it humbles and frightens me. It humbles me, Lord, because often little children say exactly what is on their minds. They are honest in a way I no longer know how to be. Often I see—shining in their eyes—the absolute faith that You are listening and will answer. It humbles me, Lord, because I am the doubter. Listening to the children's prayers sometimes also frightens me, Lord. Their words are carbon copies of hundreds of other prayers. I can tell by their eyes that sometimes they are not even thinking about the words. Prayer has become rote to them. As a teacher, Lord, never let me stifle a child's words. Help me to encourage communication—communication with You.

# WHERE HAVE YOU GONE?

*"In the same way your Father in heaven*
*is not willing that any*
*of these little ones should be lost."*

MATTHEW 18:14

Lord, teachers often hear about past students. This one went to college. This one is working for the cable company. That one is newly married. Two children and a dog for yet another one. Sometimes the news we hear breaks our hearts. I've been hearing news lately about a personal favorite of mine—all grown-up now. Lord, I offer up a special prayer. I have past students who are lost. The world has taken them by the hand and led them away from You. Find them, Lord.

# PRAY IN THE MORNING

*And pray in the Spirit on all occasions*
*with all kinds of prayers and requests.*
*With this in mind,*
*be alert and always keep on praying*
*for all the saints.*

EPHESIANS 6:18

I truly mean to pray for my classes, Lord. I even write it on my whiteboard so that every day I see the words. And sometimes I remember, but sometimes I forget. I become busy with the details. Lord, while listening to the radio this morning, I heard a statement that floored me in its simple truth. A man asked the question: Why does so great a God need us to pay Him homage—need us to pray to Him? The answer was: God doesn't require us to pray to Him because *He* needs it; we pray to Him because *we* need it. I always feel better when my prayer life is active. Keep me active, Lord. Keep the details from interfering. I do need You.

# A Rose by Any Other Name

*You, then, why do you judge your brother?*
*Or why do you look down on your brother?*

Romans 14:10

I see the name on my roster and cringe, Lord. "Oh, no." I don't know this child, but I had his sister a few years ago. I'm still finding pieces of my stuffed dinosaur whenever I open the cabinet. I threw away the books with ragged, red crayon markings on every page. I replaced all my Lite-Brite pegs. I could go on, but there's not enough time. Lord, time and time again, You remind me not to judge one of Your children based on the actions of others. And yet I do. It's human nature. I expect siblings to be carbon copies of those who came before. How boring that would be. Lord, thank You for proving me wrong over and over again. Help me to look at each child as Your creation. I pray that I never expect more or less of a student because of his or her last name.

# Put Your Hand in the Hand

*"Whoever can be trusted with very little can also be trusted with much."*

Luke 16:10

I don't remember the child's name, Father. I do remember her face, not that I'd recognize it today. She is five in my memory; she is probably entering college in real life. The first time I met her was before the school year started. Her mother brought her in for testing. I do remember she did fine and passed all the kindergarten prerequisites. After testing was over, I walked with her to the office. We'd barely taken three steps down the hallway before she put her hand in mine. Lord, there's nothing so powerful as a child's trusting touch. I'm still amazed by the emotions it evokes.

# CANDID CAMERA

*"I tell you the truth,*
*wherever this gospel is preached throughout the world,*
*what she has done will also be told,*
*in memory of her."*

MATTHEW 26:13

The first few years I taught kindergarten, I kept scrapbooks. For the children, I kept a page of pictures, samples of their work, and any correspondence from their parents (only positive, of course!), or their first awkward writings to me. In the backs of the scrapbooks, I had photos of field trips, chapel presentations, and playground days. The scrapbooks were stored in my closet. Because I taught at the same school for fourteen years, I was privileged to watch my first few kindergarten classes graduate eighth grade. That's when I dragged out their scrapbooks. I'd put them on display on graduation night. They garnished plenty of attention. Students oohed and aahed over the smiles of peers long forgotten, over missing teeth, and over awkward spelling tests. Lord, memories are a wonderful thing. I thank You for letting me be a part of so many lives. I'd like to think my presence made a difference.

# JUST ONE MORE TIME

*You always have pleasant memories of us
and. . .you long to see us,
just as we long to see you.*

1 THESSALONIANS 3:6

It's December, Lord. It's late. My feet are hurting, and I've put in a full day. I start the car and slowly put my foot on the accelerator. If I turn left, I will be home in thirty minutes. I can grab something to eat, put my feet up, plan for tomorrow, and visit with my new husband. If I turn right, I will be at my old elementary school in thirty minutes. I'll be late for the start of the Winter Program. I push the right turn signal, and off I go. I miss teaching elementary school. I miss the hugs, the noise, and the gifts of stick-figure drawings. It's dark when I enter the auditorium. I find a seat in the back, but a few of my students see me. *Miss Tracy,* they whisper. My new last name means nothing to them. Their eyes light up, and they nudge each other until all have seen me. Sometimes I wonder if I made the right choice. I cannot imagine my college students ever getting this excited just because I appear. Lord, thank You for making me a part of so many little lives.

# WHAT GOES AROUND COMES AROUND

*I planted the seed,*
*Apollos watered it,*
*but God made it grow.*

1 CORINTHIANS 3:6

I have many precious memories and more to come. I put my hand on my stomach and gently rub. I'm six months pregnant, and some teacher's future student depends on me to nourish and bear him. He won't venture into the world for three more months, and then there's five years before I need to worry about school. I'm not handing in my teacher role; I'm just adding the role of mother to my many titles. Lord, I want my child to have precious memories. I want him to learn and grow and love school. Please help me as I decide between private and public. Help me to know when to push and when to pull back. Help me to assist and not be a hindrance to the teachers who cross my child's world. Oh, Lord, thank You for the adventures of teacherhood and motherhood. Thank You for being there with me every step of the way.

# Eagerly Waiting

*"No eye has seen, no ear has heard,
no mind has conceived what God has prepared
for those who love him."*

1 Corinthians 2:9

I have name tags taped to the top of their desks, Lord. Books—math, reading, spelling, and history—are stacked there, too. I have the birthday chart up. The students *will* check to make sure I didn't miss their names. I've also written a welcome letter. It gives the parents not only the schedule, but every phone number possible—school office, church office, and my home number. It reminds parents of the special days—field trips, open house, and our first fundraiser. It's important to make sure everyone—both students and parents—understands what this year will be like. Thank You, Lord, for making sure I understand the place You've prepared for me. I know my name is written in the Book of Life. I've read Your Word; it contains math, reading, spelling, and history in it. It tells of births. It highlights special days. And it helps me understand what heaven will be like. Thank You, Lord, for preparing me.

# THE BEST-LAID PLANS

*"If anyone loves me, he will obey my teaching.*
*My Father will love him, and we will come to him*
*and make our home with him.*
*He who does not love me will not obey my teaching.*
*These words you hear are not my own;*
*they belong to the Father who sent me."*

JOHN 14:23–24

In the kindergarten classroom, when a lesson plan went awry, I'd often take the students out for a fifteen-minute recess. Sometimes I'd introduce an art project or I'd skip to the next subject. A college English professor doesn't have that option. Students come with their rough drafts, and if they are anticipating learning cause and effect, a sudden dismissal for recess just won't work. Remind me that being prepared is as much a part of the job as delivering the lesson and grading the papers. A teacher has to be prepared for anything and be able to prepare students for anything. Jesus was such a teacher. He was prepared for everything—even death. He taught lessons that were meaningful to His listeners. He taught at their level. Oh, Father, thank You for the example Jesus set. Help every teacher to strive to be the best he or she can be.

# ODE TO THE BLACK CRAYON

*"And when he finds it, he joyfully*
*puts it on his shoulders and goes home.*
*Then he calls his friends and*
*neighbors together and says, 'Rejoice with me;*
*I have found my lost sheep.' "*

LUKE 15:5–6

I want the inside scoop on the black crayon. Why does it, more than any other crayon, go missing? Do the black crayons huddle together after school and plan ways to escape? For some reason, the black crayon is the most necessary of all colors. We need black to outline and for hair. Every single color-by-number page requires a black crayon. It took me a few years to prepare myself for battle with the black crayons. Finally, I labeled a box with the word "black," and then every time a child found a black crayon, he or she got to put it in the box. I rewarded the child with a special sticker. Soon we had black crayons galore. They were jumping ship from other class-rooms and crawling to mine. Whenever there came a need for a black crayon, my classroom was the obvious place to look. Thank You, Lord, for surplus. Thank You for easy, fun solutions.

# BUT

*"But they all alike began to make excuses.*
*The first said, 'I have just bought a field,*
*and I must go and see it.*
*Please excuse me.'*
*Another said,*
*'I have just bought five yoke of oxen,*
*and I'm on my way to try them out.*
*Please excuse me.'*
*Still another said,*
*'I just got married, so I can't come.' "*

LUKE 14:18–20

Yesterday was Presentation Day, Lord. For weeks, students, in groups of five or six, had been practicing introductions, eye contact, formal speech, and so on. One young man was absent from class. His group ad-libbed his section and went on without him. Today he wants to know what he can do to make up his grade. Can he really make up this grade? After all, it was a team effort, and his team had to work around his failure to deliver—or to even contact them with an excuse. Lord, You expect us to deliver. You promise us a great reward—heaven. Lord, help me to deliver instead of making excuses.

# REFLECTIONS

*Blessed is the one who*
*reads the words of this prophecy,*
*and blessed are those who hear it*
*and take to heart what is written in it,*
*because the time is near.*

REVELATION 1:3

Lunch is an hour past and the students are reading, Lord. It's quiet time. I reach for my Bible. Looking around, I note that some are nodding off, others are staring into space, and many are reading. I wonder how many are reading because they love to read and how many are reading because I told them to. I wonder how many come from families that open the Bible in the evening. I wonder how many people are like me. I read my Bible silently, in the comfort of my bed, minutes before I drop off to sleep. Sometimes I'm so tired I forget. Sometimes I'm so tired that I do not remember what I've read a minute after I've closed Your Word. Thank You, Lord, for this quiet time to reflect. It makes me not only a better teacher, but a better child of Yours.

# Precious Moments

*Godliness with contentment is great gain.*

1 Timothy 6:6

My lesson plans for tomorrow are complete. I've finished grading the last paper and filed it away. I've no notes to write. I've no books I need to preview. For a moment, everything is in place. I have nothing I *have* to do. I look around my room. Oh, Lord, what a joyful place. I sit back and relax and just enjoy the moment—the moment You've given me. Sometimes my classroom fills me with a sense of peace, of completeness. Thank You, Lord, for breathing room and quiet time. Thank You for giving me these moments.

# LET IT BE

*"Be still, and know that I am God;*
*I will be exalted among the nations,*
*I will be exalted in the earth."*

PSALM 46:10

I know we all need emotional and physical downtime. I think some of my best memories of quiet time take place in my third-grade classroom, when the students are somewhere else and I'm standing by my big window watching the rain. Something about the way it streams down the pane makes me place my palm against the cool, smooth glass and let the daily frenetic pace slowly ebb away. Lord, I thank You for these moments of peace. Sometimes I'm not even thinking about what just happened, what I should be doing right now, or what I'm going to be doing next. Sometimes I get absolute peace from just watching the wet grass and looking for the rainbow You promised.

# REACHING OUT

*These double calamities have come upon you—*
*who can comfort you? . . .*
*who can console you?*

ISAIAH 51:19

Lord, we live during times that are anything but quiet. Some of my peers remember when a discipline problem meant talking, chewing gum, or making noise. I missed this era of school teaching. I came along when the problems were drug abuse, pregnancy, suicide, and more. As I walk down the school hallway I see a girl leaning against the wall, crying. She's in my class, but, sadly, I don't know her name—just that she often is absent and doesn't know the concept of arriving on time. My first instinct is to let her cry, leave her in the silence of the hallway, and enter my classroom to prep. It's not that I don't want to reach out, Lord. It's that I'm so afraid I'll only make things worse.

Lord, help me to take the time to reach out and know the words to say to these students who silently call out for help. I feel so unprepared for the task, but I know it's what You would do and what You want me to do.

# BADGE OF HONOR

*From the fruit of his lips*
*a man is filled with good things*
*as surely as the work of*
*his hands rewards him.*

PROVERBS 12:14

It happened again, Lord. Sparkles. They're in my hair, on my cheeks, dusting my clothes, and covering the tops of my shoes. I don't care; I still love doing art projects. I brush the sparkles off, thoroughly I think, but truthfully the sparkles will still be on my body for weeks. I'll hear from some of the parents tomorrow morning—about how sparkles look on car seats. They're like ants at a picnic. Sparkles never go away. And when people inform me, "You've got a strange bit of color on your cheek," I inform them, "Oh, I'm a teacher." That says it all. Thank You, Lord, for the sparkles on my clothes and the sparkles in my students' eyes.

# No High Heels

*"But many who are first will be last,
and many who are last will be first."*

Matthew 19:30

On class photo day, I arrange my students from shortest to tallest. It's quite a job, Lord. There are always a few who are about the same size, and when it comes to boys, they take a lot of pride in being the biggest. I use my hand to measure, and they check the soles on their shoes. I get out my ruler and measure, and they fluff up their hair. I have them stand back-to-back, and up on tippy-toe they go. Lord, You tell us it doesn't matter our station in life. You promise a reward no matter our place in line. Thank You, Lord.

# AND THEY'RE OFF

*Therefore, since we are surrounded by*
*such a great cloud of witnesses,*
*let us throw off everything that hinders*
*and the sin that so easily entangles,*
*and let us run with perseverance*
*the race marked out for us.*

HEBREWS 12:1

Our school has a wheelathon every year, Lord. It's a day all the students look forward to. Weeks before the event, students go out and find people to pledge a certain amount of money per lap. On the appointed day, each grade lines up at the starting point, and off they go. Bikes, skates, scooters, and feet pound the pavement around the school. The ultimate goal is to get the most laps (the kids really don't care who gets the most money). Teachers and volunteers keep track, and when the appointed time limit is up, students flock to find out their number so they can compare what they accomplished with their peers. We teachers are truly happiest when the race is over and no one has gotten hurt. Watch over us, Lord, as we run the most important race of all.

# Curtain Calls

*"Rise up; this matter is in your hands.*
*We will support you,*
*so take courage and do it."*

Ezra 10:4

My high school drama class is performing tonight, Lord. They know their lines. The props are in place. Everything is going exactly as planned. Then it happens. During the last ten minutes, the murderer's gun fails to fire. All my actors look at the gun. . .then they look at me. . .then they look back at the gun. It went off during *every* rehearsal. Silence fills the auditorium. Finally, the murderer looks at the victim and simply says, "Bang." She's a little confused. So he reminds her quite loudly, "You die." And down she goes. The gun was supposed to go off, Lord! But what could have been failure is really success. The audience roars. They don't know the gun malfunctioned. I've done many drama performances since, and none was as rewarding as the one when the gun did not go off. Thank You, Lord, for those moments when what we dread most turns out to be a memory we cherish.

# BEGINNING

*And she gave birth to her firstborn, a son.*
*She wrapped him in cloths*
*and placed him in a manger,*
*because there was no room for them in the inn.*

He sits there, an oldest child. He's quite an achiever and rarely causes me a problem. He's motivated. *Schoolteachers love the word motivated.* He also works hard to conquer stress. Lord, be with the oldest child. Often he carries a burden his siblings will never know.

# MIDDLE

*He and all his family were devout and God-fearing;*
*he gave generously to those in need*
*and prayed to God regularly.*

ACTS 10:2

He sits there, a middle child. He loves to be involved and seldom misbehaves. During recess, he runs at the head of the pack. He treats me well and looks out for those students smaller than he is. He is kind. *Schoolteachers love to see kindness in action.* He seeks out the accomplishments not undertaken by his older sibling. Lord, be with the middle child. Often he feels left out of activities simply because someone else can do it better.

# END

*When I was a child, I talked like a child,*
*I thought like a child, I reasoned like a child.*
*When I became a man,*
*I put childish ways behind me.*

1 CORINTHIANS 13:11

He sits there, a youngest child. *What an entertainer.* Everyone enjoys watching this social butterfly. And, oh, this child has imagination to spare. *Schoolteachers love imagination.* Lord, be with the youngest child. He worries about his accomplishments a bit more than his siblings.

# ONE IS A LONELY NUMBER

*God sets the lonely in families.*

PSALM 68:6

He sits there, an only child. Success is so important to this child. Behavior often reflects his feelings of success—both positively and negatively. This child can entertain himself—a little adult. *Schoolteachers love witnessing maturity at such a young age.* Lord, I empathize with the only child. As he is now so once was I, and I prayed for siblings every night. Lord, be with the only child. Sometimes he feels so alone.

# Knock-Knock-Knocking on Heaven's Door

*"Again I tell you,
it is easier for a camel to go through
the eye of a needle than for a rich man
to enter the kingdom of God."*

Matthew 19:24

I put the cause-and-effect example essay on the overhead and begin discussing the attributes of the five-paragraph essay with my freshman class. I chose an essay guaranteed (well, somewhat) to get the students' attention, Lord. The first paragraph introduces the effect: According to statistics, roughly 30 percent of college students will drop out during their first year. Next come three body paragraphs of causes: lack of preparation, lack of study skills, and lack of the ability to say no to temptation. It's one of my favorite lessons because the topic does get them talking. It gets me thinking, too. Lord, the Bible tells us that it's easier for a camel to go through the eye of a needle than it is to get to heaven. I'm glad I don't know the actual statistic of how many will get to heaven. I figure lack of preparation, lack of study skills, and lack of the ability to say no to temptation affect more than just my college freshmen.

# Time Flies

*"See to it that you complete the work
you have received in the Lord."*

Colossians 4:17

I am a statistic. Due to changing schools, changing majors, immaturity, and some just plain bad decision-making, it took me five years to complete college. Today's parents and students, when putting together a college budget (something I didn't do), need to consider the odds. Today most students take five years to earn that diploma. Looking back, I wish I'd been a four-year student, but, in truth, I'm pleased (relieved) that I finished. Lord, thank You for giving me the time I needed. I may be a statistic, but I'm a statistic who completed a task.

# THE BUCK STOPS HERE

*The rich rule over the poor,*
*and the borrower is servant to the lender.*

PROVERBS 22:7

Father, when I was a student, most of my friends didn't have credit cards. Today's students have, on average, five. They leave the college campus not only with a hefty school loan but with almost two thousand dollars of credit card debt. It's a frightening trend, Lord, this habit of spending money we don't have. I was well into my thirties before I truly read the credit card statement, blinked, and said, "There has to be a better way." I worry about the students who receive preapproved notices in their mailbox, and without counsel, sign their names. Lord, I'd like to pray for the students to make wise choices, but even more, I'd like to pray for the people in big business who make decisions. Encouraging debt is a bad practice. Lord, help our business leaders to lead with conscientious minds.

# BEND, DON'T BREAK

*"Through patience a ruler can be persuaded,
and a gentle tongue can break a bone."*

PROVERBS 25:15

I'm one of the instructors who "really" comments on students' papers. I mark where commas need to be, scribble in the margin about parallelism, and suggest more original voice at the end. Yes, I do compliment, too. I applaud figurative language, draw smiley faces by great sentences, and even ask for copies of the stellar papers. According to the grade gurus (yes, there are grade gurus), I'm wasting my time making multiple suggestions. Students, according to statistics, will only look at the comments if they have the opportunity to make changes. But, Lord, if they know they have a second chance, they (well, many of them) will turn in poor quality the first time. Why should they sit there with the examples I've handed out or the textbook I've instructed them to highlight in, if they know I'll show them their weaknesses? Why should they strive to find out for themselves? Lord, I want my students to grow from my guidance, and I'm always worrying that I'll make the wrong decision about approach. Send me more gurus, Lord. Help me to understand, change, and grow in my teaching.

# PRIORITIES

*Be very careful, then, how you live—*
*not as unwise but as wise,*
*making the most of every opportunity.*

EPHESIANS 5:15–16

I'm subbing for another teacher, Lord. I get to class early and write my name on the board. I set up my tools and greet the students as they come in. They seem like a nice class. About twenty minutes into the lesson, a young man walks in. He sits in the back, opens his fast-food bag, and proceeds to arrange his meal. He hasn't looked at me yet. His classmates are nonchalant, so I know that this is accepted behavior—by everyone but me. The aroma of hamburger and fries fills the room. His classmates have their books open. He didn't bring a book. He's most surprised when I ask him to leave. Lord, there are young people who work two jobs in order to attend college. There are parents who forfeit nice cars, dinners out, and cable television in order to send their children to college. I'm saddened for this young man who doesn't value an opportunity not all are given. I'm ashamed when I look back and recall the opportunities I ignored. Lord, I pray that my students will take advantage of every opportunity You place before them.

# STRANGER DANGER

*Do not forget to entertain strangers,*
*for by so doing some people have*
*entertained angels without knowing it.*

HEBREWS 13:2

Lord, I don't want to sub ever again. It's hard to enter a classroom of strangers—strangers who know each other but who do not know me. It's hard to follow someone else's lesson plan. And why can't other teachers' lesson plans resemble mine? Today I'm subbing two classes in a row, pretty much the same lesson. Class number one starts all right. Then I call on the boy who didn't bring a book to class. He's unwilling to share a book with his neighbor. In truth, he contributes nothing to the class. As a sub, I really have no power. I leave the class at the end of an hour feeling pretty much like a failure. Class number two starts all right. Again, not every student feels the need to bring a textbook to class, but at least in this class students seem willing to share. I do my best, which is all I *can* do. At the end of an hour, I dismiss the students. One asks me if I teach English 102 so she can request me for next semester. Another thanks me. Lord, maybe I will sub again. Some of these strangers have potential!

# BOOK LOVER

*But in the church I would rather speak*
*five intelligible words to instruct others*
*than ten thousand words in a tongue.*

1 CORINTHIANS 14:19

One day the sixth-grade teacher at my school called in sick. I gave up my plan period to take over her language class. She was teaching *The Giver*. I'd never read the book, so I set my first graders to quiet reading time and started skimming. It only took about five minutes, and I was hooked. Skipping lunch, I finished the book and was more than prepared to sub. Why is it some books grab my attention immediately and others take me forever? How do I get across to the children the magic of books? What words do I use? Lord, there's so much about the Bible that grabs my attention; yet there are parts that take me forever to understand. I want to understand the magic of Your book. Lord, please help me to find teachers who know how to make Your words come alive.

# CALL ME PREPARED

*Preach the word;*
*be prepared in season and out of season;*
*correct, rebuke and encourage—*
*with great patience and careful instruction.*

2 TIMOTHY 4:2

Pro: Subbing during a Sunday school class means I usually know all the students' names. Con: Subbing during a Sunday school class means that I was nabbed in the foyer two minutes after the regular teacher called in sick and two minutes before I was headed to my own adult class. I do the same thing every time. First, a scripture Wheel-of-Fortune game on the board (headed by the person who was standing next to me when I was nabbed—I mean, nabbing is fair play). While the students are playing, I try to find their student books, the attendance stickers, and I usually dash to the supply room for a craft project. Fortunately, subbing during Sunday school is usually a forty-five-minute adventure. And, Lord, sometimes I learn more during these impromptu teachings than the students do. Thank You, Lord, for the opportunity to fill in and teach Your Word. Help me to appreciate both the last-minute and full-week-notice occasions.

# PIGGY-BANK BLUES

*Be shepherds of God's flock*
*that is under your care,*
*serving as overseers—*
*not because you must,*
*but because you are willing,*
*as God wants you to be;*
*not greedy for money,*
*but eager to serve.*

1 PETER 5:2

Lord, this year the boxes of candy are almost as big as my students. It's fund-raiser time. Some students love the opportunity to hawk candy to the masses. Others shrug, knowing their parents will do the hawking. And a few parents will simply give the school a check in the amount of the candy and tell us to keep the sweets. Fund-raisers are a necessary evil. We simply have to have the funds to continue operating. Lord, guide those who have the task of handling our finances. Watch over them and give them wisdom.

# ONE DAY AT A TIME

*"However, I consider my life*
*worth nothing to me,*
*if only I may finish the race*
*and complete the task*
*the Lord Jesus has given me."*

ACTS 20:24

They've left the classroom, Lord. It's the last day of school. Moments ago, squirming bundles of energy, love, and potential were sitting in rows counting the minutes until the clock's hands stood at three. It's so quiet without them. On the first day of school, I just knew these students would never measure up to last year's students. But I have these same thoughts every year. And, always, by the end of the school year, I'm sure that this year I've had the best class in the school. Some of the students, I'll never see again. Others will adjust to their new grade and my influence will dim. A few will see me in the hall next year, and their faces will light up, and they'll run over and say, "Teacher!" I thank You, Lord, for these moments. These moments that prove, maybe, just maybe, I made a difference.

# UNTIL THE BITTER END

*Now finish the work,*
*so that your eager willingness to do it*
*may be matched by your completion of it,*
*according to your means.*

2 CORINTHIANS 8:11

Lord, children love to volunteer to help. I've had students show up at my door before school, during lunch, and after school—all wanting to help. The problem is that not all students help effectively. There are some students I seek out if I need help. There are others I create "safe" jobs for—in case they volunteer. The ones that stymie me are the ones who start, do a great job, but never finish. I'm always torn. Do I trust them this time? Or do I give them a "safe" job? Lord, how often I am like these children. You make a request. I begin the task. And when something more interesting comes along, I'm gone. Thank You, Lord, for giving me more chances. Help me to perform not just the "safe" tasks, but also the difficult, time-consuming ones You call for me to do.

# FOR ALL THE TEA IN CHINA

*I wish that all men were as I am.*
*But each man has his own gift from God;*
*one has this gift, another has that.*

1 CORINTHIANS 7:7

My students are pack rats. An old P.E. shirt, an old banana, an old spelling paper. A new pencil, a new tablet, a new P.E. shirt. Five loose crayons, four chewed erasers, three overdue library books, two pennies, and one tennis shoe. They save everything but seldom know what is really in the dark recesses of their desks. Today I have the task of digging through the desk of a student whose mother is annoyed with me for not answering her notes. Of course I didn't answer them; they're *all* in his desk—along with somebody else's missing P.E. shirt. Lord, this unique child is one of my best students, a gift from You. I ask You to watch over him and make sure he loses nothing important. Thank You for entertaining me with the contents of his desk.

# TIME STANDS STILL FOR NO MAN OR TEACHER

*There is a time for everything,
and a season for every activity under heaven.*

ECCLESIASTES 3:1

*Tick-tock, tick-tock...* I have a whole day in front of me, Lord, and precious children to teach. Their pencils are sharpened, and opportunity is in the air. I pass out their math papers and M&Ms, and off we go. First we sort by color and compare. Then we weigh the colors. Then we... Oh, look at the clock, Lord. It's time to switch to my reading lesson, but they're so enjoying this lesson and learning so much. Lord, help me to know when it's time to stay true to my teaching plan and when it's time to go with the flow.

# I NEED MORE STICKERS

*For the Son of Man is going to come
in his Father's glory with his angels,
and then he will reward each person
according to what he has done.*

MATTHEW 16:27

*Tick-tock, tick-tock. . .* I look at the clock, Lord, and it's inching past noon. I apply the last of my stickers to a beautifully colored page and stand to go to the door. Any moment, my students will return from recess. They'll bring with them pocketfuls of rocks, grubby hands, and the overwhelming smell of child. With twenty bodies, sometimes the smell of child almost sends me flying from the room. But that smell also comforts me when I'm grading papers during my plan period. It keeps me grounded and reminds me of whom I serve—in this case, children.

# RED AND YELLOW, BLACK AND WHITE

*No doubt there have to be differences
among you to show which of you
have God's approval.*

1 CORINTHIANS 11:19

*Tick-tock, tick-tock...* I look at the clock, Lord, and it's inching past two. The class begins stringing colored, round Cheerios onto strings. These will be presents for mothers to wear to a holiday party. Some mothers will sport long necklaces; these are my over-achievers. Some mothers will have average-length necklaces, with design; these are my planners. A few mothers won't be able to get the necklaces over their heads; these are my little outlaws who eat as much cereal as they string. Oh, Lord, I thank You for the uniqueness of my students—their strengths *and* their weakness.

# GETTING IT DONE

*My times are in your hands;*
*deliver me from my enemies*
*and from those who pursue me.*

PSALM 31:15

*Tick-tock, tick-tock...* I look at the clock, Lord, and it's inching past three. Where did the day go? I need more time, Lord. There's so much to do. I'll be the last one outside again. You've entrusted me with teaching my students knowledge and wisdom. I only have them for one year, and then they go off to someone else. Be with us all—every teacher. Let us strive to work together for the good of the children. Help us to use our time wisely.

# THE GRASS IS ALWAYS GREENER

*"May the LORD keep watch*
*between you and me*
*when we are away from each other."*

GENESIS 31:49

Lord, at three o'clock, I herd my children toward their destinations. They are like sheep, and I am their shepherd. Some of them head for the gymnasium. After-school care is there. My students who have mothers waiting to pick them up *long* to head into the gym and play for an extra hour. My students who head for after-school care *long* for their mothers to pick them up. So often we long for something that belongs to others. And how often do we find that what we had in the first place is exactly what we needed. Lord, help us to understand that it is Your will that we be content with our lot in life. Thank You, Lord, for supplying our needs.

# OPEN THEIR EYES

*"Do you understand
what you are reading?"
Philip asked.*

ACTS 8:30

Sometimes, Lord, I forget to ask the simple question: "Do you under-stand?" I forget that a teacher's task is not only to give new informa-tion, but also to remind students of previously learned examples. When I am impatient, Lord, remind me of the times when I've struggled to learn. Help me to remember the people who have gone over details, once, twice, twenty times with me. Let me remember the Ethiopian eunuch who said, "How can I [understand]. . .unless someone explains it to me?" And, Lord, help me to remember that while my students might not say, "Tell me, please," many of them desire a lesson much as the Ethiopian did.

# FOLLOW THE LEADER

*And the boy Samuel
continued to grow in stature
and in favor with the LORD and with men.*

1 SAMUEL 2:26

Today, Lord, two students walk past my college classroom door. One is wearing a headband with rabbit ears. The other has a raccoon tail flowing out from the bottom of his shirt. A few years ago necklaces with pacifiers were popular with my freshmen young ladies. When I taught elementary school, the little girls wanted to wear lipstick, and the boys sported rub-on tattoos. When we're young, we want to grow up. As grown-ups, we try to recapture our youth. Lord, I think of Samuel, and how his youth was spent in pursuing You. If we had such a purpose, we wouldn't need rabbit ears, lipstick, or tattoos. Lord, thank You for keeping me sane in middle age. I want neither a tattoo nor a pacifier. Keep me sane a little longer, and help me strive to grow in the knowledge and understanding of You.

# DASHED EXPECTATIONS

*"Be merciful,
just as your Father is merciful."*

LUKE 6:36

The kindergartner's parent was due an hour ago, Lord. I'm sure the birthday child is imagining the promised cake, an armload of presents, and snappy singing from all the classmates. The clock inches past the appointed time. I've had the secretary call. I'm torn. Do I have the children sing? Do I have them make cards? If I do, the parent will surely show up! The bell rings, and I send them off to P.E. In the quiet of my room, I grade papers and wait for the parent to call. Lord, sometimes my students face disappointment. Emergencies happen, and the best of intentions are shattered. I used to really hold it against the parents, these failures to follow through, but age has made me more understanding. Lord, help me simply to do my part to make each child's day the best it can be.

# Identity Crisis

*Pleasant words are a honeycomb,*
*sweet to the soul and healing to the bones.*

Proverbs 16:24

I was a fat child, Lord. Oh, I can imagine all the teachers out there shaking heads and whispering, "Chubby." And, yes, I know we can use euphemisms. We can say "cuddly," "healthy," "pleasantly plump," or "rounded." Teachers love euphemisms. We say "active" instead of "hyper." We say "restless" instead of "misbehaving." Okay, here's the truth: I was a *really* chubby child. In some ways, because I've had to conquer my self-image (and sometimes I've lost), I understand the feelings of rounded children. When I organize games, I utilize ways to guarantee that the same children are not always chosen last. I carefully word compliments to my cuddly students, hoping others will hear my words and repeat them. Lord, I pray that every child meets a teacher who is understanding of their particular need. Thank You for the teachers in my life who made me feel worthy.

# WHERE AM I?

*Your word is a lamp to my feet*
*and a light for my path.*

PSALM 119:105

"Don't talk to me like I'm one of your students," my husband says. Lord, I'm not really sure what I said to him. Maybe I asked him to eat three bites of his sandwich. Maybe I offered to tie his shoes. Sometimes it's hard to leave the elementary vocabulary in the classroom. I come home with a habit of speaking one- or two-syllable words. I come home used to giving orders and being obeyed. Lord, I thank You for giving me words to both teach my students and to communicate with my husband. Help me to always take care when choosing my words. Thank You for a husband who has a sense of humor.

# SONG OF PRAISE

*I will praise you, O LORD,*
*among the nations;*
*I will sing of you among the peoples.*

PSALM 57:9

"I've got the joy, joy, joy, joy, down in my heart!" I love hearing the voices of a hundred children raised in song, Lord. There are no words to describe the wonder. Sometimes during chapel, I stop singing so I can listen. My worldly friends are missing out on this aspect of joy. They believe that good music is played on the radio turned to such a volume that the occupants of a nearby car can also enjoy. I was raised in the church and have been singing my whole life. My husband is new to the faith and still doesn't sing in church. He's not being disrespectful, Lord; it's just that he's never opened his mouth to celebrate in song. He doesn't know how. I thank You, Lord, for the parents who took me to church where I could hear and sing Your Word.

# NO GREATER JOY

*Give thanks to the LORD,*
*for he is good;*
*his love endures forever.*

PSALM 107:1

Off they go, Lord! The school day has ended, and my students herd to either day care or waiting parents. I stand watching, making sure all find where they are going. One little girl holds the hand of the safety patrol. He starts to guide her to her waiting parents. Suddenly, she breaks free and rushes back. Grabbing me around the knees, she says, "I had a good day, Teacher." This is why I am a teacher. Thank You so much, Lord, for children who say "thank you." These words mean more to me than rubies.

# OLD TESTAMENT

# NEW TESTAMENT

# The way to Jesus Christ is simple:

### 1. ADMIT THAT YOU ARE A SINNER.

For all have sinned, and come short
of the glory of God.

ROMANS 3:23

### 2. BELIEVE THAT JESUS IS GOD THE SON WHO PAID THE WAGES OF YOUR SIN.

For the wages of sin is death [eternal separation
from God]; but the gift of God is eternal life
through Jesus Christ our Lord.

ROMANS 6:23

### 3. CALL UPON GOD.

If thou shalt confess with thy mouth the Lord Jesus,
and shalt believe in thine heart that God hath raised
him from the dead, thou shalt be saved.

ROMANS 10:9

Salvation is a very personal thing
between you and God.
The decision is yours alone.